LANDSCAPE
a common place

GW00383849

Rosamunde Codling

First published in Great Britain in 2023
by Mascot Media, Norfolk, UK.
Email: mascot_media@btinternet.com
www.mascotmedia.co.uk

A CIP catalogue record for this book is available
from the British Library.

ISBN: 978-1-7397144-3-7

Editing and layout: Mascot Media.

Printed by Swallowtail Print, Drayton Industrial
Park, Taverham Road, Drayton, Norwich,
Norfolk NR8 6RL.
Email: sales@swallowtailprint.co.uk
www.swallowtailprint.co.uk

Contents

Preface

Shortly after I was born the French writer Albert Camus jotted down in his notebook: "Write the story of a contemporary cured of his heart-breaks solely by long contemplation of a landscape." My "heart-breaks" have been few but I have enjoyed many long contemplations of landscapes, whether in real life or at the drawing board as a landscape architect and planner. These deliberations have been a major part of my life for more than 65 years, beginning as a child roaming the countryside near my home. Then followed professional training, leading to design and implementation of projects, teaching and speaking, whether to university students or six-year-olds, and academic work with long hours at a desk, struggling to convey information and ideas. Over the years I have squirrelled away anything and everything I have found that defines, comments or explores "landscape". One pleasure is the range of the material, extending from essays by the English composer Ralph Vaughan Williams to a cartoon in the local newspaper. These varied fragments might not have had an immediate effect on my work when first seen, but over the years many items in the miscellany have gradually and gently permeated my wider thoughts.

The accumulated references, notes and pictures needed sorting and sifting as there were many files on my book shelves, together with material on computer. According to the *Shorter Oxford English Dictionary*, "Commonplace books" were volumes "in which one records passages to be remembered or referred to". There is also the sense that landscape is common, as in frequent. In yet another sense, it also belongs to the community.

So I have brought together in this volume some of the many pieces that have stretched my mind, whether photographs, profound statements or humorous insights. It is not a closely argued statement that comprehensively tackles all aspects of landscape, but is offered as a stimulus to thought. I am intrigued when I find similar concepts expressed by a variety of authors, perhaps in different centuries or cultures. And then, of course, there are the conflicts – the contrary ideas about the same subject. To all these I have brought together projects and schemes on which I have worked, ranging in scale from a single field in rural East Anglia to thoughts about a whole continent.

I cannot easily divide life into categories such as work or beliefs, family or pastimes – all aspects and events, thoughts and actions mingle together, and it is this interweaving that has given delight. Relatively recently I read R. S. Thomas's poem "Those Others". It opens with the lines:

> *I have looked long on this land,*
> *Trying to understand*
> *My place in it.*

Words more eloquent than mine, and they describe my efforts over many years.

Rosamunde Codling

My foundations

I was born in the Weald, a rolling, wooded landscape straddling the borders of Kent and Sussex. Our suburban garden was limiting, but once allowed to play beyond the front gate friendships with other children expanded opportunities. Beyond the two rows of houses that were my immediate surroundings fields stretched out and provided a roughness missing from the tidiness and order of a 1930s semi. Dens were built in the hedgerows, trees were climbed, with scraped knees and scratched hands evidence of our activities.

I enjoyed my first school. The building was simple, with corrugated iron cladding a pitch pine interior. The infants sat in the front row of the first room, nearest the open fire, and as birthdays passed children gradually retreated to the back rows of the class. The process was repeated in the second room, with the eldest having the privilege of a proper desk with an opening lid rather than a table.

Our mid-morning playground was the Common, an open area of grass and woodland down the road from the school. We would assemble into a crocodile to be led by the junior teacher, with the headmistress following behind. They would sit on a bench while we played on the grass or explored a small area with a few trees and bushes.

The classroom pattern was repeated – the youngest children stayed close to the teachers, while the older ones went as far as permitted. There were no boundary fences, but limitations had been set and were instilled in our minds. "Up to the road" was one dimension and "not over the footpath" another. Looking back, it seems incredible that we were trusted to adhere to such instructions. On rare occasions there were some who dared to cross the footpath and take two steps into forbidden territory, presumably to show their bravado and disdain of the rules.

On a Wednesday afternoon the formal lesson was "nature study". We were taken on a walk over the Common to find something interesting, or we could bring items into school. We drew them before looking at a very limited supply of books to learn more about our finds. I still remember the thrill of discovering that sometimes the hop plant has a square-sectioned stem, with minute hooks that clung to the school uniform. But I suspect it was the daily visit to the Common that had the greatest influence on me. I looked at the largest tree and knew it was an oak. The bushes were gorse, but how or when I knew these names is now lost to me. Too many years have passed.

Southborough Common, Kent

Perhaps the information came from the "Observer's books" series, which cost 5/0 (the pre-decimal five shillings, a figure that became 25p) each. *British Wild Flowers* and *Trees and Shrubs of the British Isles* were among the earliest titles and were my companions in the 1950s. It was also the era of "I Spy" booklets, which at 6d (six old pennies) could be purchased with my Saturday morning pocket money rather than having to save for a hard-backed book. "I Spy" covered subjects such as *On the Farm* and *In the Country*, with detailed black and white drawings and a brief description or explanation. There was then a space to be filled when the object had been seen. As a child who enjoyed collecting and ordering, these booklets provided another source of information.

Looking back, I suspect all these factors played some part in the beginnings of an interest in landscape. As a child, I think I would have called it "the countryside" because I would be seeing it in opposition to "the town". Trying to recollect the books I had is not easy, but I remember hearing stories by Alison Uttley and Beatrix Potter. The tales were not in an explicitly rural setting, but it was obvious they were not in cities or towns. There were villages and cottages, fields with ponds, rather than streets with houses or factories. Even the hymns we sang at primary school seemed centred on the natural world, with "purple-headed mountains" and daisies as "our silver". All nudged me away from urban areas, towards woods and hedges rather than pavements and shops.

Prior to the age of about eight, the only map I can recall was a road atlas, usually kept in the car. Towns and villages were named, with railways and occasionally rivers but little more. The book held scant interest until the start of geography lessons, which generated a new mind-world far wider than the Weald, England or the British Isles. Maps came to the fore when my parents gave me *The Oxford Home Atlas of the World* on my tenth birthday. Repercussions from that book have stretched for more than 65 years, especially with regard to the last double-page spread that covered a distinct area of our globe. The Antarctic was at a scale of "one inch to 400 miles". Even then, with my vague understanding of scale, I knew the continent was large, but the aspect that fascinated me even more was an information box, unique within the book, which said:

> *Most of this continent is completely unknown and unexplored.*
> *The areas which have been seen by man are shown thus:*
> *Some of these have only been seen from the sea or from the air.*

Perhaps a tenth, or at the most an eighth, of the map was shaded brown. I would return to those pages again and again to think about such a large area that was completely unknown. My curiosity was also fuelled by the planned crossing of the Antarctic by a Commonwealth Expedition led by Vivian Fuchs and Edmund Hillary. This took place in 1957-58, but prior to that funds were needed. My primary school raised £3.12.6d, said to be the cost of a pair of fur gloves. During the Expedition we had a map of the continent on our classroom wall, and on a Monday morning we would move a pin a little closer to the South Pole. The accuracy of the pin was questionable, but the regular reminder of the polar region just added to my interest and wonder.

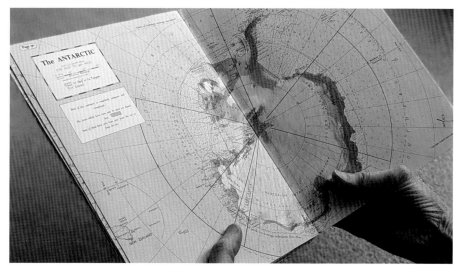

Map of Antarctica from the world atlas received as a birthday present

The consequences of those final pages in my atlas, as well as the school's enthusiasm for the Expedition, rippled through my life. My interest in the Antarctic was further stirred at secondary school by finding a biography of Edward Wilson, a medical doctor, enthusiastic naturalist and skilled artist. He was on both of Captain Robert Scott's expeditions, writing extensive diaries and technical studies, but died with Scott and three others on their return from the South Pole. During my schooldays there was no concept of role models, but over the years I have found that Wilson influenced me in several directions, including his meticulous study of birds and plants, and the outworking of his Christian faith.

A school friend was thinking about pursuing interior design as a career, and found a pamphlet describing this work. There was a short paragraph indicating that large schemes often required the collaboration of architects and landscape architects. I had an idea of the work done by an architect, but had never heard of any linkage between landscape and architecture. Designing the surroundings to a building was the most obvious pattern, but there also appeared to be opportunities to draw together schemes to meet recreational demands, or to integrate road improvements with their surroundings, or to safeguard historic parks. It seemed an interesting route to pursue, so on leaving school I went straight to college to train as a landscape architect. The four years of the course took me to a completely unknown area – the Cotswolds and the Vale of Evesham. At its end opportunities for employment were limited, and I gratefully accepted a post in Norfolk – thinking I would be there for a couple of years before moving on. I was well settled when I first heard the phrase, "Norfolk is the graveyard of ambition". The origin of the saying is debated, and, while I might dispute it, the sentiment is all too real. More than 50 years later, I still live in the county.

I worked in both local government and in private practice. Computers were gradually being introduced, with some advocating their advantages so strongly as seemingly to downplay decisions based on non-quantifiable matters. During this period the weekly *Architects' Journal* carried cartoons by Louis Hellman, an architect who lampooned his own profession with unerring eye and great humour. I was extremely encouraged by one of his offerings, which appeared as I sought to hold my own among technicians and engineers.

During my work as a landscape architect I read and continued desk exploration of polar areas, but a pivotal moment came as I turned 30. I was lecturing and teaching landscape design and planning, but the college authorities made the decision to relocate the two schools of architecture and landscape, settling them in buildings 15 miles apart. This separation of professions went against all my experience and practice; my protests were in vain, so I resigned. Academic research was then an attractive possibility and I ended up in Cambridge. "Polar Studies" gave

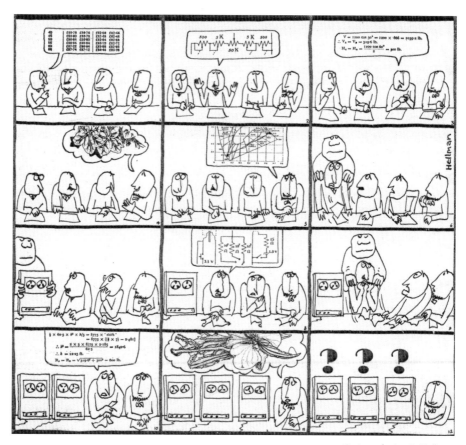

Cartoon by Louis Hellman

a wide-ranging coverage of both ends of the globe, and as a result of that year plus further research I have made two visits to the Antarctic. Landscapes of such magnitude demand thought on a completely different scale.

Work as a landscape architect and planner resulted in many years of design activity, usually beginning with periods at a drawing board or desk but then leading to outdoor activity. Within the British Isles, the scale ranged from planting schemes for window boxes in Soho to consideration of water storage reservoirs in the Wash. During one office day I had to work on both the window boxes and the Wash, but it was only later that I recognised a degree of bizarreness in their juxtaposition.

The wide estuary of the Wash is inextricably linked to the Fens, the vast, flat areas surrounding it. Over many years land has been claimed from the sea, changing lives and revising maps. Low lying and consistently level to within a few metres, farmland is edged by salt marsh which in turn merges into the sea. The "wide skies" of East Anglia seem to be even more expansive over this area of vast panoramas. Without background knowledge of the Wash water storage project of the 1970s, the two structures now seen on the ground (or in the sea, depending on the tide) appear to be forgotten remnants, casual debris from an unfinished venture.

On occasions, projects on which I've worked have developed a deeper resonance for me, involving many aspects of life, both physical and emotional. At the University of East Anglia there is a stretch of water now called the Broad, extensive enough to be seen on Ordnance Survey maps. I have to admit there is a satisfaction about that – a scheme in which I've taken part is clearly visible on a nationally published map. From a historical point of view, its name is a misnomer – but more on that later. The Broad was constructed over a lengthy period but without payments being made between the university as client and the contractor, an unusual situation and unique in my experience. Of all the projects in which I've been involved, this seems to be the one with the greatest human impact and the longest-lasting repercussions. Many years after its completion, there emerged a tenuous link to a story of human bravery and dignity. Happenstance, maybe, but real enough to me.

Closest to home is the Moat, a modest 3.4-hectare field of heavy Norfolk clay with a near-circular mediaeval moat in the centre. We purchased the field with the idea that it would provide us with an alternative to a restricted city garden. Initially I worked at a drawing board, planning tree planting, but for the past 30 years there has been hard physical on-the-ground labour rather than delicate annotation of drawings. Quite clearly history plays a major part in the venture, but within our family lives it has brought together the responses of children to landscape as well as consideration of our long-term futures.

Despite differences in size, the Wash and the Fens, the Broad and the Moat have affinity. They all lie in eastern England, an area a traveller does not pass through

The Wash and Fens, looking west past the mouth of the Nene to Gedney

The Moat and island, Norfolk

on the way to somewhere else. Antarctica is similar. It has to be a definite destination; it can't be chanced upon by a casual traveller. To link it with East Anglia probably seems incongruous, especially in terms of size – the polar region is more than 14 million square kilometres, the Moat about 0.034 of a square kilometre. Expressed in another way, Antarctica, including its islands and ice shelves, is more than 40 times the size of the British Isles, and the Moat is a very small field in one county of our country. At varying levels I am acquainted with these parts of our globe, and from them and through them I continue to explore the concept of landscape.

The Broad, University of East Anglia, Norfolk

Landscape foundations: a connection with place

Should we talk about landscape or landscapes? Is there a difference? My immediate response is that there is no simple answer that applies to every situation. I have to talk about landscapes of Wales or Ireland or England or Scotland, because each country has many different areas, each with their own characteristics. A landscape is one of those tracts, a distinct locality that can be described if necessary, so if we talk about an expansive region, such as a country, it is inevitable that there will be a collection of such areas resulting in the use of "landscapes".

Studying the spectacle, looking and thinking as a discipline, results in using the singular form of the word. The Dutch word *landscap* was introduced in the late 16th century by art dealers and critics, who used it to describe a picture of inland scenery, especially in Holland. Its origins in painting cannot be forgotten, but it has moved on to wider realms.

A British postage stamp issued to commemorate the 50th anniversary of the discovery of DNA shows two jubilant scientists holding up the last piece of their Genome jigsaw puzzle, but it appears they have not realised that their completed jigsaw forms just one piece of an even larger puzzle. Landscape is like that. One piece of the jigsaw is described by an expert such as a geologist, explaining how underlying rocks influence the shaping of the land, or an ecologist relating the development of flora and fauna. Historians give accounts of successive human actions affecting overlying layers. They, and many others, contribute their skills, sometimes making a passing reference to other disciplines, but all too often covering only one small part of a much wider whole.

Genome **The End of the Beginning**

Postage stamp marking the 50th anniversary of the discovery of DNA: "Genome: The End of the Beginning" by cartoonist Peter Brookes

Landscape surrounds us, simultaneously giving us information through multiple senses. Both our central and peripheral vision are in play, and often we have more material than we can immediately use. We are compelled to be involved in the whole but we might then consciously or unconsciously disregard aspects. We cannot passively observe, and inevitably our personal emotions or beliefs come into play. The writer V. S. Naipaul understood this: "Land is not land alone, something that simply is itself. Land partakes of what we breathe into it, is touched by our moods and memories."

We all have cultural patterns that we consciously or unconsciously accept. They are the pigeonholes we use to understand concepts that might otherwise seem too abstract or complex. We may be influenced by national characteristics, the society in which we live, our upbringing or any one of the many factors that have affected our lives. Our senses respond to inputs from the environment around us, and while these may be impossible to measure or calibrate in any way we recognise the whole experience.

When I was lecturing on the landscape architecture course I found details of a project given to first-year students. They were asked to imagine an individual, forced to isolate because of an infectious disease, in accommodation with a garden that had been specifically designed for them. The teaching programme gave a selection of characters from which students could choose – I can only remember the list included a Tudor merchant and a present-day aristocrat. The garden was intended to aid their recuperation by giving them surroundings they would recognise and in which they would feel at home. Little did anyone realise that about 45 years later the whole nation would be in that position of isolation, with "lockdown" confining us to our homes. Gardens became critical for the wellbeing of many people, but there were others, in flats or tight urban settings, who lacked such facilities. The project was developed to stretch ideas, rather than to demonstrate design capabilities. As first-year students, they were being encouraged to widen their thoughts about underlying factors that influence design, whether historical contexts or social mores, let alone personal preferences and emotions. These aspects now probably come under headings such as environmental psychology.

In America, a husband and wife partnership worked extensively trying to understand responses to the natural environment. Stephen Kaplan wrote: "There have been numerous efforts to identify the crucial aspects of the human reaction to landscape, to get to the heart of the matter, as it were... [What] I would like to propose is a functional approach, a view of what people are trying to do. When people view a landscape, they are making a judgment, however intuitive and unconscious this process may be. This judgment concerns the sorts of experiences they would have, the ease of locomoting, of moving, of exploring – in a word, of functioning – in the environment they are viewing."

In summary, responses would always be varied and wide-ranging: "Different people will extract different information from the same environment, and different environments offer different kinds of information to the same person." I found that an initially confusing statement and remember that as a student I was always wanting clear directions, but landscape never offers simplistic approaches. Certain functional aspects are capable of solutions – paths have to go where people need to go, their surfaces have to be suitable and so on, but even clear-cut issues offer varying design possibilities.

Childhood experiences have an importance that is often forgotten, or at least underestimated. "People attach to the type of landscape in which they grew up... People are marked by the living creatures and natural environment they encountered during childhood because understanding and mastering our surroundings has been necessary for human survival." My childhood landscapes were the woods and copses of the Weald, followed in my student days by the hills of the Cotswolds. Moving to Norfolk gave me the first opportunity to visit the coast more frequently; and now, if given a choice, I would gravitate towards a seashore, whether the dunes and low cliffs of East Anglia or the harder, rocky margins of our island. So while my early life rooted me firmly among trees, my delight has been extended to the sea edge. However, I see this as an augmentation, rather than as a replacement, of earlier inclinations. I suspect I appreciate the options available at any one period rather than yearning for an ideal.

But reading about others and their preferences has confirmed the importance of experiences when young. The writer and politician John Buchan spent much of his childhood summers with his grandparents in the Scottish Borders. In an introduction to Buchan's autobiography, the literary scholar David Daniell wrote: "The secret springs of his life were clearly in those Border uplands, in the relation of a spiritual world, whether Wordsworthian or Platonic or Calvinist, to an intensely personal, far-spread landscape, known with all the senses, and intellectually and spiritually grasped. He knows his landscapes from the fall of the rivers, and understands experiences from the effects of climbing hills." Buchan was a prolific writer, and after finishing his autobiography he began a book about fishing. Only two chapters were drafted before he died, but in these he identifies himself as "one who was under the spell of running water. It was in terms of them that I read the countryside. My topography was a scheme of glens and valleys and watersheds." He goes on to say that for the whole of his life this pattern remained, and whether in southern Africa, the eastern seaboard of the United States, or Canada, he "read" the landscape by rivers and their valleys.

This was a remarkably strong framework that I do not possess. I am not one who seeks the high hills and mountains, perhaps because I had no experience of them until my late teens. When in prison from 1943-45, the German theologian Dietrich Bonhoeffer wrote: "In my dreams I live a good deal in nature, in the woods and meadows of Friedrichsbrunn or on the slopes – the slopes from which one can look beyond Treseburg to the Brocken. I lie on my back and watch the clouds sailing past on the breeze and listen to the murmur of the wood. What a profound effect such memories of childhood have on the human character. I cannot imagine myself ever having lived up in the mountains or by the sea; it just does not fit my nature. It is the hills of central Germany... which belong to me and have made me what I am... perhaps my midland hills are bourgeois, in the sense of what is natural, not too high, modest and self satisfied, non-ideological, content with concrete realities, and above all not given to self advertisement. It would be very tempting to pursue this sociological treatment of nature further some day." He never had the opportunity to explore these thoughts, as shortly afterwards, in 1945, he was executed by the Nazis.

Almost at the same time as Bonhoeffer was writing, similar "midland" views, but this time about England, were expressed by H. E. Bates, a prolific writer on the countryside. "I was born among the pastures: on that large East Midland plain that takes in Northamptonshire and its nine adjoining counties... If you reckon it in terms of impressive landscape features it is probably also the dullest plain in England. Its hills, until you come to the boundaries of the Chilterns in the south, the Cotswolds in the south-west, and the real hills of Nottinghamshire and Derbyshire in the north, are not much more than bumps made by generations of gnats on the green skin of the land... It is a pattern of sobriety... At twenty I disliked the Midlands; at twenty-five I hated them; at thirty, having left them, I began to understand them. I began to see how fortunate I had been to have been brought up on that diet of clay pudding which is as fundamental to English scenery as Yorkshire pudding is to English dietary. I feel that I was fortunate for this reason. A man brought up in Devon or the dales of Yorkshire or the Westmorland lake country is often found never to have any real taste in any other scenery. He has been brought up too well; he has never known what it is to be poor. Whereas a man brought up on a flat plain diet, as I myself was, has a taste capable of being educated in any kind of scenery."

The intensity of childhood memories was strongly expressed to me by a friend, raised in Norfolk and living there for the majority of her life. In her seventies she moved to Australia to be near some of her family. She made a passing comment about not missing East Anglia; and, when pressed to explain, wrote:

"Belonging to a place is an enriching, perhaps an essential, part of human experience. I sometimes have to explain that I can't miss Norwich and Norfolk because it's built into me. It's my birthright – as indivisible from me as my DNA. I don't think this identification is peculiar to me. I believe that it's something everyone experienced before this footloose age. That old Music Hall song 'I belong to Glasgow, dear old Glasgow town… But when I get a couple o' drinks on a Saturday, Glasgow belongs to me' says the same thing.

"Kipling puts it more elegantly in 'Sussex by the Sea':

God gave all men all earth to love,
But since our hearts are small,
Ordained for each one spot should prove
Beloved over all…

"This connection with place goes much deeper than just being fond of somewhere. It becomes a shared identity:

So to the land our hearts we give
Till the sure magic strike,
And Memory, Use, and Love make live
Us and our fields alike –
That deeper than our speech and thought,
Beyond our reason's sway,
Clay of the pit whence we were dug
Yearns to its fellow-clay.

"Feeling like this is quite different from homesickness. Perhaps it's something you have to live a long time to experience. Flecker's anguished longing '…shall I never…be home again?' was written when he was 27. Browning was 34 when he wrote: 'Oh to be in England now that April's there…' Perhaps the sure magic had not had time to strike."

Childhood memories are clearly an integral part of our understanding of landscape, but lessons learnt later develop our ideas. Almost 2,000 years ago a Stoic philosopher suggested that it is not events, but our opinions about them, that cause us suffering. Hopefully, responding to landscape should not lead to suffering, but although Epictetus was thinking about personal circumstances his ideas are relevant to thoughts about landscapes. It could be followed by the much quoted statement from Proust's monumental novel *Remembrance of Things Past*: "The real voyage of discovery consists not in seeking new landscapes but in having new eyes."

I have found the more I recognise and understand my responses, and the more I know about landscape, the greater the enjoyment. I can also use these acquired tools to think about landscapes beyond my reach, whether areas of our planet or beyond our immediate world to the moon and other parts of the solar system. Older texts often provide short, sometimes sweet, and even humorous statements about landscapes. Thomas Fuller was a clergyman, historian and prolific writer living through and surviving the turbulent eras of Charles I, the Commonwealth and the restoration of Charles II. "Know most of the rooms of thy native country before thou goest over the threshold thereof. Especially seeing England presents thee with so many observables."

Fuller's "observables" were colourfully described by John Ray (1627-1705), writing about 50 years later. Sometimes described as "the father of natural history", Ray travelled extensively throughout the British Isles and then Europe, writing many biological works. "...the *Earth* should be made... with so great variety of parts, as Mountains, Plains, Vallies, Sand, Gravel, Lime, Stone, Clay, Marble, Argilla [potter's clay] &c. which are so delectable and pleasant, and likewise so useful and convenient for the breeding and living of various Plants and Animals; some affecting Mountains, some Plains, some Vallies, some Watery Places, some Shade, some Sun, some Clay, some Sand, some Gravel, &c. That the Earth should be so figured as to have Mountains in the Mid-land parts, abounding with Springs of Water pouring down Streams and Rivers for the necessities and conveniencies of the Inhabitants of the lower Countries; and that the Levels and Plains should be formed with so easie a declivity as to cast off the Water, and yet not render Travelling or Tillage very Difficult or Laborious. These things I say, must needs be the result of Counsel, Wisdom, and Design. Especially when (as I said before) not that way which seems more facile and obvious to Chance is chosen, but that which is more difficult and hard to be traced, when it is most convenient and proper for those nobler Ends and Designs, which were intended by its Wise Creator and Governor. Add to all this, that the whole dry Land is for the most part, covered over with a lovely Carpet of green Grass and other Herbs, of a colour, not only most grateful and agreeable, but most useful and salutary to the Eye: and this also decked and adorned with great variety of Flowers of beautiful Colours and Figures, and of most pleasant and fragrant Odours for the refreshment of our Spirits and our innocent Delight."

A similarly prolific writer was Daniel Defoe: "In travelling thro' England, a luxuriance of objects presents it self to our view: Where-ever we come, and which way soever we look, we see something new, something significant, something well worth the travellers stay, and the writer's care." A few year later, in the latter part of the 18th century, the landscape designer Capability Brown is reputed to have refused work in Ireland because "I have not yet finished England".

In one sense I can echo Capability Brown's words. I have had projects in several parts of England; but, with regard to knowledge of the whole, there are far too many areas of this one country, let alone the other parts of the British Isles, that I have not seen, despite a lifetime of looking. As a teenager I was allowed to cycle with friends around a small area of the Weald. Later, the Cotswolds were on my student doorstep, then my first-ever visit to Norfolk led to work and long-term living. This progression has probably been a pattern followed by many. Study and work takes us to initially unknown places, which gradually become familiar.

To counteract any reluctance to look beyond known boundaries, a few years ago I cut two pages from the front of an old road atlas. Intended as route planners for England and Wales, the map showed cities and a few towns, main roads and major rivers, but little else. I shaded those areas I did not know, exposing my ignorance of large parts of the country. My husband did the same; then we drew up a list of areas to visit. Apologies had to be given to Wales, Scotland and Ireland – the thought was that we should explore by visits of a few days, and as Norfolk was our home the outer reaches of the British Isles were beyond consideration and would have to be treated as a major holiday.

Over the years we wandered through quite a few of our identified areas: the Wirral; Market Harborough and Northampton; Margate and the North Kent coast; Lichfield and Walsall; Hartlepool and the Durham coast; the Essex coast south of the Stour; Silverdale and Arnside to the south of the Lakes. Many areas remain to be explored: the Lincolnshire Wolds, the Chilterns, the Vale of Belvoir, Cannock Chase and other areas of the Midlands that have been traversed on the way to other places, but otherwise ignored.

However hard we try, there will always be aspects of landscape that we will never be able to state or classify in a systematic way. Techniques for the analysis of landscapes were being discussed and developed in the 1960s and '70s, often with great confidence that comprehensive methods were being developed. One American landscape architect, R. Burton Litton, pointed out gaps and sounded a warning note: "Descriptive literature suggests that seasonal aspects of landscape or its apparent modification by weather or light may indeed make the most indelible impressions upon the observer. Reference to the 'ephemeral landscape' has been a personal attempt to recognize this idea. Additionally, the sequential movement of the observer through the landscape, both in time and space, may profoundly alter a person's sense of scenic values. The reasons for omitting these several things from evaluations are simple enough. We do not know how to do it; or prospects for agreement are poor. Here is another set of interesting dilemmas."

When I first read Litton's paper, I appreciated his honesty and was glad that a respected figure in the profession had spoken so clearly. Many years later I read his obituary, which identified another facet that is too often forgotten. His university colleagues wrote: "Burt had a keen eye for the common landscape and encouraged his students, friends, and colleagues to gain an appreciation and a stewardship responsibility for ordinary landscapes." The tendency always seems to be to ignore the "average" and only consider the "special".

Litton's observations about fleeting glimpses, or movement through the landscape, are still pertinent. Sometimes they have been identified more clearly by poets or writers, such as Edward Thomas. In the early years of the 20th century he wrote lyrically about Hampshire in June: "The hawthorn bloom is past before we are sure that it has reached its fulness. Day after day its warm and fragrant snow clouded the earth with light, and yet we waited, thinking surely to-morrow it will be fairer still, and it was, and the next day we thought the same and we were careless as in first love, and then one day it lay upon the grass, an empty shell, the vest of departed loveliness, and another year was over." This is a small part of the "ephemeral landscape", an element that colours our thoughts and preferences and which should not be ignored or forgotten.

Inevitably there are those who do not share enthusiasms or concerns about landscape. *The Cornhill Magazine* provided a forum for many Victorian writers, and in 1882 an essay by Robert Louis Stevenson was published. Stevenson wrote: "No human being ever spoke of scenery for above two minutes at a time, which makes me suspect we hear too much of it in literature." The essay was reprinted many times, and a copy seems to have found its way to the Antarctic as about 30 years later Robert Falcon Scott included this quotation at the end of one of his manuscript journals of this, his first, expedition. He makes no further comment, either in his daily entries or after his recording of Stevenson's words – he simply reproduces them. Yet the diaries or journals of many members of the expedition show that they wrote extensively about their surroundings, possibly attempting to convey the backdrop of their lives to family and friends. Edward Wilson, head of the scientific staff, wrote in his diary for 23 August 1902: "We had the whole of Erebus island spread out in front of us, and it was a very beautiful sight indeed. One of the thoughts that strikes one oftenest I think is what people at home would give to have a glimpse of such a sight." Wilson was also a skilled draughtsman and watercolourist, so in addition to his writing he produced many landscape drawings, sketches and paintings.

Perhaps Oscar Wilde was advocating a middle way: "It seems to me that we all look at Nature too much, and live with her too little. I discern great sanity in the Greek attitude. They never chattered about sunsets, or discussed whether the shadows on the grass were really mauve or not. But they saw that the sea was for the swimmer, and the

North Kent, looking towards Essex

Hartlepool, looking towards Teesside

sand for the feet of the runner. They loved the trees for the shadow that they cast, and the forest for its silence at noon."

Landscapes are for living in, and many of their components meet our material needs. But there is more – landscapes are part of our lives, places where values and emotions co-exist, giving us a different form of sustenance not met by other means. There is a succinct summary by David Lowenthal, geographer and historian, that identifies our personal involvement: "Landscape is everyone's fundamental heritage. It is all embracing and unavoidable. It inspires and shapes much of what we learn and do. Landscape is where we all make our homes, do our work, live our lives, dream our dreams. Yet for each of us it means something different, formed by our unique collective and individual experiences... Awareness of landscape involves active participation, however motionless the beholder. Wind and weather, light and shadow, clouds and sky, seasonal foliage, the disposition of birds, animals and people make each glimpse a new scene, even when seen repeatedly from the same spot. Moreover, landscape changes as we move through them; each step, each turn of the head, engages new vistas. So much depends on our physical interaction that no static scenic consensus can adequately reflect it."

An ephemeral aspect: the smell of wild garlic by a path, Gower, Wales

Landscape and history

The link between landscape and history cannot be explained in a single statement. I could cover many pages quoting from some of the numerous attempts that have been made, but all fall short. Nevertheless, descriptions can help, perhaps because we find it more comfortable to have a summary in our minds, a backdrop that at least provides a setting for adding or incorporating other ideas.

In the last 50 years or so, one approach has been to describe landscape as a "palimpsest", from the Greek and Roman practice of using wax-coated tablets, which allowed for modifications to be made by scraping the surface clean and starting again. In mediaeval times, parchment and vellum could also be reused in this way. I have found that suggestion helpful – the idea that landscape is layered, perhaps with earlier parts remaining, sometimes in their original form, sometimes modified or even eliminated. New patterns might be added, but it is not usually possible to superimpose a totality on the land. Arthur Bloom, author of a seminal book about landforms, suggested a similar device, relating to geological processes: "As in a manuscript one or more older texts can sometimes be read beneath the latest words, so in the description of landscapes, previous processes and stages of development can be recognized beneath or within the landforms that are now being shaped." Although writing about one country, the historian Christopher Taylor takes the thought further: "The English landscape is made up of many interrelated features. Its basic skeleton has been formed from the rocks, moulded by time, etched by rivers and ice, and clothed with a mantle of green vegetation, but superimposed on this is man's work. No part of England is untouched by man's endeavours over thousands of years."

"Man's endeavours" covers every human activity, from governments at a national level down to the actions of an individual. Even a cursory exploration of one of our family homes and its surroundings revealed its place in history. We were living on the edge of Norwich city centre, in a terraced house with a small garden, a convenient and enjoyable home overlooking the Cathedral and the Close, and within walking distance of the city centre. It stood beside the road that was once the mediaeval thoroughfare linking Norwich to Great Yarmouth and close to Mousehold Heath, which had provided extensive grazing near to the city. The house stood on a slope, with the river Yare below, the navigable route to the coast and the North Sea. In Victorian times, and possibly earlier, chalk excavations near the house supplied building materials such as lime for mortar and flints for walls; and later, during World War II, caves in the quarry had been used

Caistor St Edmund, Norfolk

as air-raid shelters. Within a few hundred metres of a Victorian terrace, evidence could be found of a history beginning in geological eras and continuing through mediaeval developments and later industrial activities to events within living memory.

When I was lecturing, one of the slides I frequently used was of the landscape near Caistor St Edmund on the outskirts of Norwich. My original slide has deteriorated, so I returned to the area to remind myself of the reasons for my earlier choice. In simple chronological terms, the longer grass on the right, under the Scots pines, covers a possible Iron Age site. In the middle distance lies the site of the Roman town of Venta Icenorum, which began to grow some time after the Iceni revolt of AD60/61, before reaching its peak in the 4th century, then suddenly declining in the 5th. The mediaeval church of St Edmund, seen amidst the trees, was built within the boundaries of the Roman site, using some Roman materials in its construction. Beyond are 20th-century 400KV pylons, feeding a major electricity station which serves the city of Norwich; and, just below the horizon, the Southern Bypass, completed in 1992, swings round the edge of the city. So one relatively small area demonstrates at least 2,000 years of landscape history. For students, perhaps new to the idea of chronological complexity, it was a helpful example.

While we were living in Norwich, I was lent a book by Charles Kingsley, *Madam How and Lady Why: or, First Lessons in Earth Lore for Children*. It was published in 1879, and the second part of its title gives a fair indication of its contents. Kingsley was an able children's author, especially with regard to "nature study", and one of the episodes he relates seemed particularly applicable to thoughts about landscape:

"When I was your age, there were no such children's books as there are now. Those which we had were few and dull, and the pictures in them ugly and mean: while you have your choice of books without number... But mere reading of wise books will not make you wise men: you must use for yourselves the tools with which books are made wise; and that is – your eyes, and ears, and common sense.

"Now, among those very stupid old-fashioned boys' books was one which taught me that; and therefore I am more grateful to it than if it had been as full of wonderful pictures as all the natural history books you ever saw. Its name was *Evenings at Home*; and in it was a story called "Eyes and no Eyes"; a regular old-fashioned, prim, sententious story; and it began thus: – 'Well, Robert, where have you been walking this afternoon?' said Mr. Andrews to one of his pupils at the close of a holiday.

"Oh – Robert had been to Broom Heath, and round by Camp Mount, and home through the meadows. But it was very dull. He hardly saw a single person. He had much rather have gone by the turnpike-road.

"Presently in comes Master William, the other pupil... terribly dirty and wet he is: but he never (he says) had such a pleasant walk in his life; and he has brought home his handkerchief... full of curiosities.

"He has got a piece of mistletoe, wants to know what it is; and he has seen a woodpecker, and a wheat-ear, and gathered strange flowers on the heath; and hunted a peewit because he thought its wing was broken, till of course it led him into a bog, and very wet he got. But he did not mind it, because he fell in with an old man cutting turf; who told him all about turf-cutting, and gave him a dead adder. And then he went up a hill, and saw a grand prospect; and wanted to go again, and make out the geography of the country from Cary's old county maps, which were the only maps in those days. And then, because the hill was called Camp Mount, he looked for a Roman camp, and found one; and then he went down to the river, saw twenty things more; and so on, and so on, till he had brought home curiosities enough, and thoughts enough, to last him a week.

"Whereon Mr. Andrews, who seems to have been a very sensible old gentleman, tells him all about his curiosities: and then it comes out – if you will believe it – that Master William has been over the very same ground as Master Robert, who saw nothing at all.

"Whereon Mr. Andrews says, wisely enough, in his solemn old-fashioned way, – 'So it is. One man walks through the world with his eyes open, another with his eyes shut, and upon this difference depends all the superiority of knowledge which one man acquires over another... While many a vacant thoughtless youth is whirled through Europe without gaining a single idea worth crossing the street for, the observing eye and inquiring mind find matter of improvement and delight in every ramble. You, then, William, continue to use your eyes. And you, Robert, learn that eyes were given to you to use.'"

Kingsley said that some might find the original story "old-fashioned, prim, sententious", but it told a tale that I hope children can still understand. He was quoting from an earlier book published in 1793, *Evenings at Home* by Anna Laetitia Barbauld and her brother Dr John Aikin. A couple of hundred years had passed since then, but its intention to encourage exploration of the countryside is still relevant. A friend once described her walks as "daisy-banking", a pattern that allowed for frequent stops for any reason appropriate at that moment, whether birdwatching or contemplation, botany or conversation. Her description echoed Master William's activities. Nowadays I also follow this model, rarely covering vast distances, but frequently stopping, so as to listen or gaze or examine. It is a development of the pattern gradually learnt as a child, initially encouraged by my primary school – curiosity at every level, whether distant views of the horizon or minute insects circumnavigating lichens on an exposed rock.

When I was at college studying landscape architecture, the only landscape historian was W. G. Hoskins, a revered figure who wrote the seminal work on the subject, *The Making of the English Landscape*, first published in 1955. Hoskins recognised his limitations and later wrote: "The material evidence of the past lies all around us, if only we can construe the language it is speaking... I have tried to construe this language; and even if I do not know all the answers (and I do not) I have at least tried to offer clues to the alphabet." In 1972 there was a BBC television programme with Hoskins as presenter, and after that he compiled a shorter but heavily illustrated book, *English Landscapes*. The end of the Introduction in that book illustrates the interwoven, sometime complex, relationships between landscape, social history, art and literature, and also highlights the insights offered by people in different generations. Hoskins wrote:

"Constable – that beloved and most English of painters – quotes:

'It is the Soul that sees; the outward eyes
Present the object, but the Mind descries.'"

Then he adds a sentence that could be the theme of this whole book insofar as I have been successful in conveying it:

'We see nothing till we truly understand it.'

Unpacking Hoskins' conclusions reveals three individuals, working in their chosen media and spanning 160 years. The Suffolk poet George Crabbe (1754-1832) was a close observer of rural affairs and the landscapes of East Anglia, and did not hesitate to portray the grim realities of peasant life in an economically depressed area. The couplet used by Constable was the opening of one of Crabbe's *Tales in Verse*, published in 1812.

He was going beyond mere vision, suggesting that mental and emotional responses are not only different from simple observation, but are more important. Just over 20 years later Constable was giving four lectures on the history of landscape painting at the Royal Institution in London. After quoting the two lines by Crabbe, he added a third, presumably his own: "We see nothing till we truly understand it."

Some have suggested that Constable was considering purely physical aspects of what we see – understanding that a house in a landscape has walls that are hidden from an observer, or that a distant ball is spherical, even though there is not enough detail to confirm this. But Constable, nearly 60 and coming to the end of his life, was speaking to a sophisticated and educated audience – so surely his words indicate a deeper and more searching insight. Hoskins certainly took them this way. In his eyes, his subject had no confines, and he was pursuing anything and everything that had contributed or influenced the scenes he saw with his eyes.

This one short quotation displays the intricacy of landscape. In a few lines that span 170 years, the words of a socially aware poet are taken by a painter, who adds a further notion, before their thoughts are appreciated and applied by a historian to landscape. I am sometimes a spectator, sometimes an explorer, not only of the actual scenes of the land, but of the thoughts and concepts given by those in many other disciplines.

"Taking up the mantle" is not the most appropriate figure of speech to describe the successor to a landscape historian such as Hoskins – probably "wearing the gum boots" would be more applicable. *The History of the Countryside* by Oliver Rackham, a Cambridge historian and ecologist, was published in 1986, going beyond the alphabet and beginning to lay the foundations of the language's grammar.

Rackham used the word "countryside" rather than "landscape", perhaps to differentiate his book from Hoskins' earlier work, but it also avoids entering into the then growing, and sometimes heated, discussion about the multitude of meanings of "landscape". Countryside has a gentler, all-embracing remit; as such, nothing is barred from consideration. More recently I heard it used in a story being read to under-fives in an inner-city library. They were asked if they knew what it meant. None answered, so the librarian said it was "a big garden that's got out of control". To adults, a definition that could be challenged; but, within the context of the story and the probable experiences of most of the children, it fitted.

In conveying the essence of his extensive research to a wide readership, Rackham took a mischievous pleasure in challenging widely held views such as that the oak trees of the Weald were decimated so that the navy could build ships for the Armada. I attended one of his lectures that he opened with a collection of such statements, delivered with a serious demeanour but followed by a long pause. Then he declared that all his earlier pronouncements were factoids, something that "looks like a fact, is respected as a fact, and has all the properties of a fact except that it is not true". The rest of the lecture went far beyond superficial or cursory pronouncements.

Rackham's painstaking work resulted in a totally justifiable authority throughout his writings. He railed against historic landscape destruction but chose to convey the message with a degree of humorous despair: "The landscape is like a historic library of 50,000 books. Many were written in remote antiquity in languages which have only lately been deciphered; some of the languages are still unknown. Every year fifty volumes are unavoidably eaten by bookworms. Every year a thousand volumes are taken at random by people who cannot read them, and sold for the value of the parchment. A thousand more are restored by amateur bookbinders who discard the ancient bindings, trim off the margins, and throw away leaves that they considered damaged or indecent. The gaps in the shelves are filled either with bad paperback novels or with handsomely-printed pamphlets containing meaningless jumbles of letters. The library trustees, reproached with neglecting their heritage, reply that Conservation doesn't mean Preservation, that they wrote the books in the first place, and that none of them are older than the eighteenth century; concluding with a plea for more funds to buy two thousand novels next year."

Any landscape in the British Isles has a history that can be explored, by both fieldwork and desk study of available sources. Gaps are inevitable but do not always distract or diminish an overall understanding. Geological eras lead to prehistory periods, and then to relatively recent history, revealed by books, maps or manuscripts. I often explore and question, seeking at least an overall picture, but on occasions I allow the landscape to wash over me. Constable's statement, about truly understanding the prospect before us, may be the ideal, but there are circumstances where acceptance of lesser knowledge is appropriate, when we allow our immediate responses to dominate.

During a recent cross-country journey from East Anglia to Wales, a traffic jam halted our car somewhere in Northamptonshire. A 20-minute delay followed, but in that time we had the opportunity to look more carefully at the landscape around us. To the north, beyond the central barrier and adjacent carriageway, the land rose gently to a low hill, with cattle grazing on the grassed field. Beyond, and situated just below the horizon, wind turbines turned in the breeze. The grass cover of the field varied, with darker strips alternating with lighter shades of green. I think we were seeing the gentle curves resulting from "ridge and furrow" ploughing, probably dating from mediaeval times. Rackham goes into detail about typical dimensions, but we did not have the opportunity to measure the double curves we were seeing. For me, despite the frustration of delay, the enjoyment of the landscape before us was increased by the thought that it probably showed the activities of man over many hundreds of years.

The Covid-19 pandemic has become part of the history of the whole world. In the United Kingdom, each of us has experienced restrictions placed on our lives, and has had to work in resolving, or coping with, the many difficulties. In the spring of 2020,

Northamptonshire landscape, north of the A14

during the early days of the first lockdown, the BBC Radio 4 programme *PM* asked listeners to write 400 words about their lives. All the submissions would ultimately find their way into the British Library as a *Covid Chronicle*. After some thought, I wrote:

"The lane to the recycling centre is narrow, running between the old gravel quarry and the marshy ground that surrounds a meandering stream, grandly called a river on the maps. Normally cars speed down the road, often with clouds of dust rising from the rough surface; or, if wet, with mud splashing from the potholes. But at the moment it is a peaceful route out of the town, ultimately leading to a path across a vast field. It offers the chance of an hour's walk, with few encounters other than an occasional dog walker or parents with reluctant children following behind.

"Two railway lines have to be crossed. The first is the link between the 'heritage railway' and the main line, so now it is silent; but the second is active, linking Norwich to Cambridge and the Midlands. Crossing needs care, even with the reduced service. The trains that pass appear to be empty, suggesting that lockdown is being respected.

"Both the lane and the railway are part of history. 'Strayground Lane' is the official name, but often local people simply say they are going down to Strayground. Presumably it led to a parish field that was used to hold wandering animals before they were reclaimed. The railway was the first line between Norwich and London, opened in 1845. So when walking today there are reminders of earlier times – the farming community and the industrial age of the 19th century. Now we are adding to history, a period that will be named and remembered 'the Covid-19 pandemic'.

"But in walking along Strayground there is an encouragement that I have missed when driving to the recycling centre. I have only noticed it now, in the peaceful afternoons. Between the road and the old quarry is a bank, and on its slopes are elms, growing with vigour in the spring sun. They are probably English elm, a tree that was almost wiped from the landscape in the 1970s by the invading fungus called, probably unfairly, Dutch Elm Disease. These thickets will not grow into magnificent trees, but they continue the presence of elm in our landscape.

"So today we see life after the devastation that occurred 50 years ago. We hope the recovery from our present pandemic will be far shorter and that skilled scientific work will lead to protection from this Coronavirus. Meanwhile, we are able to enjoy a quiet Strayground, and take encouragement from signs of continuing life."

Looking back at this piece, in a simple way it sketches just part of the history of a short lane, itself only a fraction of a modest community. The physical features of that small area of land are not striking or impressive and have been extensively modified by the gravel extraction. The vegetation is not exceptional but still contributes to the landscape. Reasons for the name of the lane deserve further exploration in the town's archives, as does the development of the two railway lines. So far more could have been explored and written about, but in a restricted number of words I tried to capture and convey moments in my own life – the geographical place I happened to be in as well as its past history. The piece was not selected for broadcasting but the thought that it will be a contribution to a national archive is comforting – a recognition that individuals can contribute to history.

The road to Strayground, Norfolk

Two complex characters: Darwin and Ruskin

An admission first: I do not claim to understand Charles Darwin or John Ruskin in all respects, but as two 19th-century writers they have pushed me to think harder about landscape. On my bookshelves is a set of Ruskin's *Modern Painters*, five volumes with a total of more than 1,800 pages. I have dipped into these, and also into his other writings, but acknowledge that I have not read everything from cover to cover.

Both Darwin and Ruskin wrote about landscape, possibly at almost the same time. Many of the issues they raised have become critical points in the study of landscape and its importance in the planning procedures of the 20th and 21st centuries – the understanding of, or efforts to put a value on, "beauty"; the importance of the environment to wellbeing; and the tunnel-vision of different disciplines, which often leads to conflict. Looking at their writings has been both constructive and perplexing, but Darwin's Notebooks especially deserve close study. His thoughts and musings show the breadth of his vision and willingness to explore ideas.

Darwin and Ruskin apparently met several times. When Darwin (then aged 28) returned from the voyage in the *Beagle* he presented a paper at the Geological Society in London. That was his first meeting with Ruskin, then 17 and a student at Oxford. In later years Ruskin severely criticised Darwin, but contemporaries remarked that, despite their differences, they greatly enjoyed each other's company. One academic has suggested that Ruskin's problems were not with Darwin the man, but with Darwin<u>ism</u>, the summaries or comments drawn up by others of the original work *The Origin of Species*, written in the 1850s.

Clive Wilmer, an enthusiastic advocate for Ruskin, has suggested that the younger man belonged "to the same tradition as Darwin" but grasped the wider implications all too well. "Darwin was pointing out a road that Ruskin had no wish to travel down. In the things he loved most – the flowers, the creatures, the clouds and the mountains – he could see nothing but the struggle for survival, the outcome of which could only be... senseless, degrading death."

Throughout the 19th century, probably because of Darwin's writings in particular, the so-called conflict between science and religion raged. Much has been written about the dispute, but it "deserved to die, because it was not really between science and Christianity at all, but between mistaken views of each; and that the true scientific spirit expresses something which is not only a possible but necessary ingredient of a fully Christian faith. Christian faith is not credulity; like scientific belief in one respect at least, it is trust based on experience and on testimony judged reliable.

It differs from scientific belief not in its standards of truth but in its mode of origin."

The online facsimiles of Darwin's Notebooks are fascinating as his seemingly frantic handwriting – with copious corrections and amendments – illustrates the torrent of thoughts passing through his mind. Darwin's *Notebook M: Metaphysics on Morals and Speculations on Expression* was in use from 1838 to 1856 so the exact date of the note about "scenery" is unknown, but his thoughts spill out with varied punctuation and shortened spellings. I have made some simplifications:

Analysis *of pleasures of scenery.*

There is absolute pleasure independent of imagination, (as in *hearing* music), this probably arises from (1) harmony of colours, & their absolute beauty, (which is as real a cause as in music) from the splendour of light, especially when coloured. That light is a beautiful object one knows from seeing artificial lights in the night. From the mere exercise of the organ of sight, which is common to every kind of view, as likewise is novelty of view even old one, every time one looks at it...

2^d Form, some forms seem instinctively beautiful as round, ovals... Again there is beauty in rhythm & symmetry, of forms... this gives beauty to a single tree, & the leaves of the foreground either owe their beauty to absolute forms or to the repetition of similar forms as in angular leaves... this symmetry & rhythm applies to the view as a whole. Colour & light has very much to do, as may be known by autumn, on *clear* day.

3^d Pleasure association *warmth, exercise, birds singings.*

4th. Pleasure of imagination, which correspond to those awakened during music. Connection with poetry, abundance, fertility, rustic life, virtuous happiness. Recall scraps of poetry; former thoughts, & in experienced people. Recall pictures & therefore imagining pleasure of imitation come into play. The train of thoughts vary no doubt in different people: an agriculturist, in whose mind supply of food was evasive & ill defined thought would receive pleasure from thinking of the fertility; a geologist have ill-defined notion of land covered with ocean, former animals, slow force cracking surface etc truly poetical; the botanist might so view plants & trees. I am sure I remember my pleasure in Kensington Gardens has often been greatly excited by looking at trees as great compound animals united by wonderful & mysterious manner. There is much imagination in every view. If one were admiring one in India, & a tiger stalked across the plains, how one's feelings would be excited, & how the scenery would rise. Deer in Parks ditto.

Darwin's identification of individuals interpreting the same scene in ways unique to their disciplines or preferences is all too frequent. We see a place or prospect through our eyes and, perhaps inevitably and probably imperceptibly, we slip a filter across our sight that influences our subsequent assessment. Sometimes it is a specialism such as geology or ecology, but it can also be a less-defined preference that might be due to influences such as upbringing or experience. It is easier to present a limited perspective on any issue, but landscape usually demands and deserves a holistic approach.

When Darwin wrote "trees as great compound animals united by wonderful & mysterious manner", I wonder if he had an inkling of the complexities of relationship that we are now only just beginning to understand. He knew of the writings of the German geographer Alexander von Humboldt, who explored South America between 1799 and 1803, observing the associations between many different forms of life. Darwin picked this up and developed the concepts. About 30 years later he, too, visited South America, during the voyage of HMS *Beagle*. The last paragraph of *The Origin of Species* illustrates the intricacies of his observations: "It is interesting to contemplate an entangled bank, clothed with many plants of many kinds, with birds singing on the bushes, with various insects flitting about, and with worms crawling through the damp earth, and to reflect that these elaborately constructed forms, so different from each other, and dependent on each other in so complex a manner, have all been produced by laws acting around us."

I appreciate his identification of the interrelationships, whether found in Kensington Gardens or in South America, but I have reservations about his use of "laws" as an account of the processes. It is a far too definite and confident term to describe complexities that are still being examined. As one example, more recent research has revealed an amazing shared fungal network between trees. Not too surprisingly, it has been named the Wood Wide Web. In one study, a single Douglas fir was found to be linked to 47 other trees. If, in turn, they are linked to yet other trees, the network is staggering in its complexity.

I recollect an occasion when as students we were required to carry out a very simple ecological survey in a Worcestershire wood. Digging into the soil underneath a coppiced hazel revealed bluebell bulbs, roots of grasses and perennial plants, as well as surface mosses and lichens attached to decaying leaves and wood. We were seeing only visible evidence, and that was tangled enough to our untrained eyes. To know now that there is a microscopic world of fungi, probably linking a wide variety of plants, deserves considerable further thought.

An unexpected interpretation of Darwin's "imagination in every view" came one spring when I was being driven through villages and farmland on the borders of Suffolk and Essex. With others, I was taking part in a short bell-ringing course, an intense period of theory combined with practice in local churches. On the way to one tower there were large, undulating fields, mainly wheat, bounded by desultory hedges, occasional thatched cottages, sometimes with intricate pargeting – the decorative plaster patterns applied to walls. The four of us in the car were talking casually, but gradually the conversation was led by the recollections of an elderly local man. He didn't speak of field patterns, or the state of the crops, but only about the bells in local churches. We passed through a village that clearly had a mediaeval street pattern, together with exceptional buildings, but for him the community was identified as having "the best light 6 in the county". He was referring to the weight of the bells, and for them to be classified as "the best" implied that they were both tuneful with pleasing reverberations as well as being hung so as to make them relatively straightforward to ring. A casual mention of the emerging wheat immediately reminded him of the achievements of three brothers from a milling family who took part in a lengthy peal of Oxford Treble Bob Major while still teenagers in June 1914. For him, the wheat-dominated landscape only served as a reminder of an earlier generation of ringers. Further conversations reinforced this proclivity towards bells – he continually responded to his wider surroundings through the pursuit of Stedman's Principle or Cambridge Surprise Major. His landscapes were fashioned by bells and constrained by church tower walls.

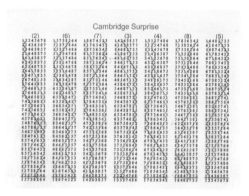

Cambridge Surprise Major – an eight-bell method

Ruskin wrote copiously about landscape and the beauty of living things, especially in their relationship to landscape painting. In one of his passages (cited by the poet Matthew Arnold as a good example of Ruskin's prose), he begins: "Gather a single blade of grass and examine for a minute, quietly, its narrow sword-shaped strip of fluted green. Nothing, as it seems there, of notable goodness or beauty. A very little strength, and a very little tallness, and a few delicate long lines meeting in a point – not a perfect point neither, but blunt and unfinished, by no means a creditable, or apparently much cared for example of Nature's workmanship; made, as it seems, only to be trodden on to-day, and to-morrow to be cast into the oven; and a little pale and hollow stalk, feeble and flaccid, leading down to the dull brown fibres of roots. And yet, think of it well, and judge whether of all the gorgeous flowers that beam in the summer air, and of all strong and goodly trees, pleasant to the eyes or good for food – stately palm and pine, strong ash and oak, scented citron, burdened vine – there be any by man so deeply loved, by God so highly graced, as that narrow point of feeble green... Consider what we owe merely to the meadow grass, to the covering of the dark ground by that glorious enamel, by the companies of those soft, and countless, and peaceful spears. The fields! Follow but forth for a little time the thoughts of all that we ought to recognise in those words. All spring and summer is in them, – the walks by silent scented paths,– the rests in noonday heat... the life of sunlight upon the world, falling in emerald streaks, and falling in soft blue shadows... soft banks and knolls of lowly hills, – thymy slopes of down overlooked by the blue line lifted sea."

When reading this passage my thoughts immediately turned to Albrecht Dürer's watercolour with the accurate but unromantic name *Large Piece of Turf*. Ruskin wrote about one blade of grass; Dürer illustrated the complexity of just one clump, showing hundreds of blades together with several other species. I strive to consider landscapes as intricate networks of a multitude of factors: in one sense an audacious and presumptive task, but perhaps because of personal experiences and patterns it is inevitable that I make the attempt.

Ruskin had no such qualms, and wrote extensively about landscape – usually

"Large Piece of Turf" by Albrecht Dürer

with reference to paintings, but also covering his view about actual places. He also felt it reasonable to compare and contrast landscapes. This perspective was shared with Darwin, who noted in his *Beagle* diary: "There is a growing pleasure in comparing the character of scenery in different countries, which to a certain degree is distinct from merely admiring their beauty." In taking this approach, both men ignored Wordsworth's earlier judgement that such evaluations were "injurious to genuine feeling".

The fourth book in my set of *Modern Painters* runs

to more than 400 pages, and is called "Of mountain beauty", which clearly shows Ruskin's preferences. Nevertheless, he writes: "Putting Lincolnshire, Leicestershire, and one or two such other perfectly flat districts aside, there is not an English county which I should not find entertainment in exploring the cross-roads of, foot by foot; yet all my best enjoyment would be owing to the imagination of the hills, colouring, with their far-away memories, every lowland stone and herb."

Residents of both Lincolnshire and Leicestershire have every reason to challenge Ruskin on his observations regarding the flatness of their counties. The Wolds in Lincolnshire and Charnwood Forest in Leicestershire may not be mountains, but their undulating landscapes should not be snubbed. At least Ruskin admitted his bias for more dramatic scenes. He went on: "I know that this is in great part idiosyncrasy; and that I must not trust to my own feelings, in this respect, as representative of the modern landscape instinct; yet I know it is not idiosyncrasy, in so far as there may be proved to be indeed an increase of the absolute beauty of all scenery in exact proportion to its mountainous character, providing that character be *healthily* mountainous. I do not mean to take the Col de Bonhomme [a pass in the Vosges Mountains of France] as representative of hills, any more than I would take Romney Marsh as representative of plains; but putting Leicestershire or Staffordshire fairly beside Westmoreland, and Lombardy or Champagne fairly beside the Pays de Vaud or the Canton Berne, I find the increase in the calculable sum of elements of beauty to be steadily in proportion to the increase of mountainous character; and that the best image which the world can give of Paradise is in the slope of the meadows, orchards, and corn-fields on the sides of a great Alp, with its purple rocks and eternal snows above; this excellence not being in any wise a matter referable to feeling, or individual preferences, but demonstrable by calm enumeration of the number of lovely colours on the rocks, the varied grouping of the trees, and quantity of noble incidents in stream, crag, or cloud, presented to the eye at any given moment."

Ruskin was greatly admired by Edward Wilson. When a student at Cambridge in 1894, Wilson was awarded a prize and chose five volumes of Ruskin. However, his admiration for the man did not prevent gentle criticism. In Wilson's view, Ruskin's influence could have been greater had he not put "people's backs up by telling them that they wanted leavening and he was going to do it".

In their time, the work of both Darwin and Ruskin generated controversy. The tendency now is to examine the disputations raised by their critics, and forget to examine the actual writings of the two men. Perhaps we resist putting aside the time for this – Ruskin's inability to keep to one subject or train of thought is far from today's accepted patterns. But the willingness of both men to explore ideas, even if beyond their initial disciplines, is something I admire and have tried to follow.

Portrayal of landscape

A book about landscape and landscapes is not the real world, and can only point to some of the issues about looking and experiencing, whether in real life or by representations. Remembering that the word *landscap* originally referred to paintings, it is inevitable that thought turns to different patterns of portrayal, despite knowing that any depiction will be limiting in some way or another. Multiple factors combine to form a landscape, and efforts to capture all at once will not succeed. Yet words can enlarge an understanding, or a painting might capture an aspect that has been overlooked. Rather than identify limitations, I find it more helpful to recognise that different forms of representation can amplify or augment the whole. Much has been written about landscape, whether art or literature, and I greatly enjoy exploring such offerings, but now I prefer to delve into one or two notions that have stayed with me.

Between the two World Wars half a dozen or so "walkers with literary gifts" were active in the English landscapes. Joan Thirsk, a social and agrarian historian, wrote: "The writers who set these features in a frame became almost household names. H. J. Massingham, C. Henry Warren, Adrian Bell, and H. E. Bates are among the best remembered from this period, encapsulating the spirit of a region in their books. H. J. Massingham... perceived two significantly different attitudes to landscape among his writers, some seeing it as a work of art, and being content to describe and enjoy its aesthetic beauty, others seeing it as the work of people, and wanting to see the painters as well as the pictures. Massingham confessed himself to have been once a disciple of the first school, looking only for scenic distinction, but was then converted to joining the second, wanting to see the people who had made the scene." I continue to explore that generation, once called nature writers, as well as those publishing now. More recently, the discipline has earned the title "environmental humanities", drawing not only from literature, language, history and the arts, but also from philosophy, anthropology and cultural studies. The range is wide, and offers great enjoyment, especially when restrictions prevent actual access.

Towards the end of World War II a slim book of poetry was published under a simple, descriptive title: *English, Scottish and Welsh Landscape: 1700-c.1860*. Verse was chosen by John Betjeman (who described himself as a "poet and hack") and the Irish poet Geoffrey Taylor. They wrote:

"We were given three thousand lines for a *representative* anthology of landscape poetry. We confined ourselves to the most prolific period, 1700 to about 1860... We chose inland scenery and concentrated on country subjects. We demanded that the poet should have obviously looked at and loved what he described... Cunningham's conventional landscapes have been well described... as 'like a vast oil on a dining-room wall in an eighteenth-century mansion – the kind that goes with the house because it is too big for the auctioneer to sell'. The wooden passage from Dodsley is like an inn signboard: Bampfylde is a Morland: Goldsmith is some not very good picture, but so famous that it could not be omitted: Crabbe has the freshness of a Cotman water-colour: many of the lesser-known writers round the turn of the century are like the copper engravings or Bewick cuts which, no doubt, adorned some of their works. As for these lesser-known people – quiet Georgian rectors, village schoolmasters, peers in their libraries looking across the park, Victorian drunks and reformers and escapists – they are the reason for the book. They were recording landscape from the distant view to the cascade in a wet cart rut, with a love and observation men are just beginning again to appreciate."*

These paragraphs give us a portrayal of landscapes via a circuitous but enjoyable route. To begin with, poets selected words to convey their response to scenes, and many years later their work was selected for an anthology, suggesting that they achieved a degree of success in their endeavours. In explaining their choices Betjeman and Taylor have, sometimes humorously, compared the verses with objects and artworks of about the same era. They give the image of a painted inn sign for Dodsley – probably a simplified and perhaps clumsily painted representation. Crabbe is commended as having "the freshness of a Cotman water-colour". Other artists are then mentioned, so the selectors assume their readers would have a knowledge of painters and engravers of the era. It is definitely a meandering prelude to the volume, which is possibly why it is headed "Apology" rather than the more usual "Introduction" or "Preface".

There is an additional pleasure in the book – it includes a generous number of John Piper's lithographs portraying landscapes. Black-and-white reproductions are sometimes disappointing, but Piper's ability to use the medium results in strong, dramatic images.

Dylan Thomas was many years outside of Betjeman and Taylor's remit, but several of his poems convey his surroundings in a vivid way. Perhaps it is helped that Laugharne, the Welsh coastal town where he lived for a couple of years, standing on the estuary of the River Taf, is rich in strong landscape features – hills, woods, saltings and coastal mudflats, all influenced or varied by the continuous changes of the tide

---

* *The poems mentioned by Betjeman and Taylor: John Cunningham (1729-1773) "A Landscape". Robert Dodsley (1703-1764) "Agriculture: a poem" – Middlesex. John Bampfylde (1754-1796) "On a Wet Summer" – Devon. Oliver Goldsmith (1728-1774) "The Deserted Village". George Crabbe (1754-1832) "The Borough" – Suffolk.*

and weather. In just a few lines from "Poem in October" he conveys his surroundings, perhaps nostalgically, as he was writing some years after he had left the town:

Blackbirds and the sun of October
Summery
On the hill's shoulder,
Here were fond climates and sweet singers suddenly
Come in the morning where I wandered and listened
To the rain wringing
Wind blow cold
In the wood faraway under me.

Pale rain over the dwindling harbour
And over the sea wet church the size of a snail
With its horns through mist and the castle
Brown as owls.

It is said he walked up the hill flanking the west side of the estuary, to the right of the castle. Whether this was the exact location of this poem or not, the importance of the landscape to him is clear. He ends in hope:

O may my heart's truth
Still be sung
On this high hill in a year's turning.

I stayed in Laugharne for a few days, and in that time was able to walk most of the local footpaths. The town is compact, an entity within a complex and ever-changing landscape. There was not only variable weather, and the seasonal signs bearing witness to the onset of autumn, but the twice-daily tidal cycle over the wide banks of sand and mudflats. I knew only a scant number of works by Dylan Thomas, but it was one of the occasions when I have been very conscious of links between my surroundings and a specific creative person. At Aldeburgh in Suffolk, Benjamin Britten's "Sea Interludes" can easily be recalled, or A. E. Housman's "A Shropshire Lad" poems when beside the River Teme or in places such as Clun. Here, Thomas's "Poem in October" lived more vividly when remembered on the hill beside the estuary of the Taf.

Laugharne and the estuary of the Taf

One form of media can be used for many different purposes. A photograph can be an artwork in its own right, but will be different from one taken to be used as a postcard, which in turn will differ from an advertisement. Postage stamps are not book illustrations, field sketches are not completed paintings. So it is not only the image that has to be considered but also the original purpose for its existence and the time it was produced. Similarly, if the same landscape is described at varying times, or under changed circumstances, it will be understood in a different way. The scene of a crime or the presence of war will darken the panorama. Once it might have been a warm, homely view, but because of events it is then seen as hostile or grim.

This book contains photographs – a two-dimensional image is used as a representation of a multi-dimensional environment. Many accept this without question. There are numerous academic papers that attempt to evaluate landscape preferences by showing photographs to a selected audience or to a random crowd, and then using the responses to develop rankings. I am uncomfortable with this approach. Can a single photograph, or even a video, convey enough information on which to base a reasonable assessment?

There has been at least one research project that tested "real" against "representation". A sample of students followed a walk through an area of woods and fields, rating their preferences and articulating their emotions at specific places. Two weeks later the same group took part in a laboratory test with the same sites represented by photographic slides. The combined results of these procedures led the researchers to conclude that people did not respond similarly to an onsite landscape experience and a simulation in the form of photographs. Their responses about preferences were more complete when they were on the walk, rather than looking at images. It was concluded that the multi-sensory dynamics of landscapes needed to be considered. This was academic work, a controlled study, and it supported my apprehension about the sole use of photographs for assessment.

There has been long-standing unease about ways of representation and our responses. In the 18th century the landscape gardener Humphry Repton became embroiled in a lengthy debate with two acquaintances, Uvedale Price and Richard Payne Knight, who belonged to the picturesque school of thought. Essays, letters, pamphlets and poems flowed from the pens of the combatants, and one of the many points at issue was the relationship between landscape painting and landscape gardening.

Repton identified significant differences between a picture and a natural scene. In the 1793 *Red Book for Holme Park* (one of the volumes he prepared for his clients showing by sketches and annotations the "before and after" views of their estates) he listed the major differences between a painting and the scene from nature. The painter works from a single viewpoint, which is very different to being able to look at a scene from a variety of positions, and the view is always more extensive than a painting can capture. He also pointed out that a painter can manipulate the light in his work, rather than accept natural conditions which vary throughout the day. Remarkably, almost all of the issues he summarised corresponded to those of environmental psychologists of the 20th century.

A variation of this "reality versus representation" debate involved the composer Ralph Vaughan Williams. In 1920 he wrote an essay attacking the then current opinion that a musically educated person would be content to appreciate the art by reading scores rather than hearing music. Vaughan Williams described this as a "fallacy", and used appreciation of a landscape to support his case: "A musical score is like a map. The expert map reader can tell fairly exactly what sort of country he is going to visit, whether it is hilly or flat... whether it is wooded or bare... but can he experience from a map the spiritual exaltation when a wonderful view spreads before his eyes?"

Towards the end of his essay, he wrote: "Would Ulysses have been obliged to be lashed to the mast if the sirens instead of singing to him had shown him a printed score? When the trumpet sounding the charge rouses the soldier to frenzy, does anyone suggest that it would have just the same effect if he took a surreptitious glance at *Military Sounds and Signals*?" The match is far from perfect between score and audible music, photographs and the real world, but Vaughan Williams' trenchant approach highlights some of the issues.

The lot of a landscape artist has never been easy. Thomas Rowlandson's hand-coloured aquatint *An Artist Travelling in Wales* gave an 18th-century view. Leaving wife and family behind, in driving rain the intrepid artist grimly pursues his calling over treacherous landscapes. Just over 100 years later a diary entry by Edward Wilson, the talented amateur artist who accompanied Captain Scott on both his expeditions,

AN ARTIST Travelling in WALES.

conveyed yet more of difficulties encountered. He, too, had left his wife behind and had to cope with weather conditions far more extreme than those found in the British Isles. On the first occasion he recounts his difficulties he was at sea, en route to the Antarctic: "Painting a bird which is swinging through 30° every few seconds is trying too. Things won't stay as you put them. Your water is hung on a hook, your paper pinned to a board and you hold your paint box. You yourself are wedged into the bunk cupboard and kept there by a boot on the chest of drawers opposite. You put your paint box down to settle a wing for the thirtieth time and down it rattles and the paints go all over the cabin. You jump to save the paint box and the corner of your board tilts the water tin off the hook and it empties into a drawer full of clean drawing paper; while a running drip takes the opportunity of coming down from the skylight on to your painting of the bird that you are doing."

Wilson devised a hooded drawing board that gave him some protection as he drew. When in the Antarctic, the distraction of breaking seas or running water was replaced by severely low temperatures and howling winds. Nevertheless, he produced both precision pencil drawings and sketches, which on occasions he would annotate with notes about colours, so that finished works could be produced when back at base.

There was no official photographer on Scott's first expedition in *Discovery* (1901-1904) but Skelton, the chief engineer, took on the work and was in charge of the darkroom. By the time of Scott's second visit with *Terra Nova* (1910-1914) there was a far greater understanding of the publicity potential and value of photographs, so a skilled photographer, Herbert Ponting, was appointed. He preferred to be called a "camera artist" – an indication of his approach and expertise. His still photographs and film from a portable movie camera recorded the expedition to a very high standard. In his diary, Wilson made the pertinent comment about Ponting: "He has got some very marvellous work done down here. He is really a master at getting pictures by photography." The two men clearly had a deep respect for each other's abilities.

Our understanding of any painting or photograph is inevitably conditioned by the context in which we are seeing it. Moving from the southern continent to northern Europe, John Berger's book *Ways of Seeing* reproduced Vincent van Gogh's painting *Wheatfield with Crows* at the bottom of a right-hand page, with the text: "This is a landscape of a cornfield with birds flying out of it. Look at it for a moment. Then turn the page." On the top of the next page, the same picture appeared, this time with a caption: "This is the last picture Van Gogh painted before he killed himself."

The author went on to say: "It is hard to define exactly how the words have changed the image but undoubtedly they have." Words can change images and landscapes.

Taking this approach to Antarctica, it would be straightforward to present a similar "picture with later explanation". If a photograph showing the Beardmore Glacier was captioned, "The glacier used by Scott for his expedition to the South Pole, which led to his death together with his four companions", responses to the magnificent but daunting landscape would probably be unfavourable. Words have coloured reactions. If the same picture had been captioned, "The route used by both Shackleton and Scott to gain access to the polar plateau", the glacier's place in history would have been acknowledged without an emotive edge. When I was working on conservation issues relating to the continent, there were calls from the polar community to designate particular areas because of their outstanding qualities such as "aesthetic values" or "wilderness". I had reservations about "ranking" features or areas, unless clear criteria could be stated for such selection, but suggested that if the polar nations saw an essential need for designations there were factors that could be helpful. If it was considered necessary to single out one glacier above all others, I proposed the Beardmore. Shackleton and Scott's choice gave the feature an historic value in addition to its mere glacial mass.

Wandering through less frequented presentations of landscape has been interesting. "Stiffeners", the term used by both printers and tobacco companies, were an essential part of cigarette packaging in the mid- to late-19th century. Printed pictures and information on the cards first occurred in the mid-1870s in America, and inevitably the practice spread to Britain. In 1891, just over a decade later, free education for five- to ten-year-olds began, and for a short time children from poorer homes became more literate than their parents. Attempts to assess the impact of ephemera such as cigarette cards have to be speculative, but this expansion of education, together with improved printing techniques, helped to increase accessibility of the printed word for those on lower incomes. While standards varied greatly, some cigarette cards could genuinely be seen as miniature reference works, offering coloured illustrations and informative text. Cards averaged 70-110 words in three or four sentences, usually resulting in well over 20 words per sentence. I find it worrying to realise that this is more than the pattern currently adopted by some British newspapers.

Two "Polar Exploration" sets, each of 25 cards, were produced by John Player & Sons in 1915 and 1916. By the time of issue there had been well over a dozen major expeditions, not only from European countries but also from America, Japan and Australia. The cards mention only Scott's two expeditions, plus Shackleton's visit and the Norwegian party led by Amundsen. The emphasis is on human exploits, with well over half of the Antarctic cards covering transport (mainly sledges in one form or another, but also ships) or the work being done (taking observations, setting up camp and care of the ponies and dogs). The message of the cards is clear – man has explored the southern polar continent, lived there and, despite a few problems, has reached the extremity of the Earth. Hardships and difficulties of life in the Antarctic are covered only briefly.

Shortly after the polar cards were published, Player's published another set called "Gems of British Scenery". It is interesting to see how landscape was portrayed at the time. The set of 25 cards covers the whole of the British Isles, although well over three-quarters of the cards show England. The illustrations are carefully planned, often with strategically placed small boats or foreground groups (whether people or sheep) to aid artistic composition. Every card in the set includes water, whether the sea, lakes or rivers, and only about a quarter have no man-made features. The language of the cards is as picturesque as the illustrations: "a perfect dream of beauty" is followed by "mingling of sylvan loveliness and old-fashioned rusticity". The influence of literature is also apparent. The first six cards are all of North Devon, the

Cigarette cards 4 and 18 from "Gems of British Scenery" issued by John Player & Sons

setting of *Lorna Doone*, which had been published in 1869 and led to a surge of popularity for Exmoor.

The set displays a romantic, even nostalgic, view of the British Isles. Comments made about factors that go to make up the countryside, such as geology and vegetation, can only be described as superficial, and the overall impression is that the beautiful scenery of the British Isles should be visited and appreciated. There is no suggestion that any man-made structure detracts from the landscape, as the buildings shown in the cards, whether Balmoral Castle, Tintern Abbey or North Devon cottages, are all seen as contributing to the view. Indeed, "the view" comes through as a major factor. A little is said about "walks and drives", but the emphasis is on visiting to enjoy at a single scene. In a later generation, all the images would be classified as "chocolate-box" choices, but at the time they all conformed to the title of the set, "Gems of British Scenery".

But even chocolate-box pictures can be manipulated by a few words. Some time ago, during a warm summer, newspapers related the trial that followed the disappearance of two young children. Photographs were published of the area where their bodies were ultimately discovered – the edge of the Fens where it joins the sandy Breckland. One such picture depicted rural England with harvested fields extending to the horizon and small copses, all bathed in sun. The accompanying text recast the image. Described as a "gloomy, forsaken corner", with reeds growing in "dank patches" and "an unwelcoming path" being "swallowed up by the blackness of thick woodland", the pastoral idyll became a horror story.

On a far lighter note, I have enjoyed seeing one word turned into a landscape. In 1972 a flicker book by Chic Taylor was published – 20 small pages that can be rapidly flipped through to suggest a moving image. The letters of the word "landscape" are eroded, as if by rain, and pieces fall, forming hills. As this process is nearing completion, clouds develop and the end result is a picture – a two-dimensional representation of the idea suggested by the original word. A small, entertaining item, hardly profound, but it gently reminds me that, in the end, thought and theory are best seen in an actual reality.

In the middle of the 17th century someone wrote about the art of limning, now an archaic term describing work on illustrations in manuscripts, or sometimes simply paintings. The writer said: "Landscape is nothing but Deceptive visions, a kind of cousning or cheating your owne Eyes, by our owne consent and assistance, and by a plot of your owne contriving." I have not seen the manuscript containing these words, which is held by the Bodleian Library, so I do not know the author or the context in which they were written, but I see them as a challenge.

To begin with, I am always alerted when the phrase "nothing but" is used, as the writer or speaker has chosen to limit the scope of their pronouncements and inevitably there are more factors that need to be considered. But I think it would be profitable to debate the statement, to query the concepts of "deception" or "cheating". As it stands, I would agree with at least part of the statement. It is our "owne" responses that count, our personal reactions, whatever medium is used to portray or convey the landscape. This gives us freedom, the possibility to find delight and pleasure in innumerable and unrestricted ways.

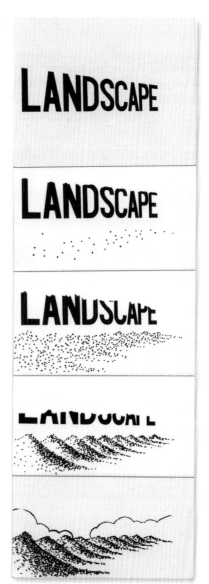

The erosion of "Landscape" by Chic Taylor

Postcards of Erratics:
The Burren, Ireland; Whernside, Yorkshire; Skye, Scotland

People in the landscape

Can landscape ever be separated from people? The single word is a human response to land, and any exploration of its meaning often arrives at the doors of scholars, whether of philosophy, philology, aesthetics or psychology. Their arguments are almost always interesting, sometimes enlightening, but often confusing. Rather than immersing ourselves in such investigation, perhaps a simpler approach is to think of people "in" the landscape.

Even if "in" the landscape, we sometimes turn our backs to the view. The development of the mobile phone with a camera led to the birth of the "selfie". It is easy to create many pictures, then select one (which probably shows the self-photographer to best advantage) to share with friends. The irony is that for a shot with a specific setting, a selfie has to be taken with the subject's back to the view. The landscape is being seen as the background to the resulting photograph, an accepted setting but not the most important part of the picture. In essence, the self-photographer is saying: "I'm here but now I'm turning away and ignoring the reason for me coming here."

Turning your back on the landscape is not new. In the late 18th century the Claude Glass – a small convex mirror with a tinted surface – was used by painters and travellers to admire a scene from a chosen viewpoint. The user had to face away from the view, and then hold the mirror to one side, so as to see a reduced and simplified version of the landscape behind them. Many of the resulting drawings or paintings used people simply as compositional aids. Their enjoyment of the landscape, or involvement in it, was immaterial.

George Seddon (1927-2007) was an Australian environmental scholar who delighted in crossing boundaries of academic disciplines. During his career he chaired faculties in English, geology, history and the philosophy of science, and environmental sciences, as well as working in the community. One of his essays was a study of paintings and photographs from the 19th century to the present that showed the view of the Australian city of Perth from Mount Eliza in Kings Park (the historic vantage point from which members of the community could look over the city, the recreational area for all to enjoy):

"There are figures in nearly all the views from Mt Eliza until the 1930s, when they disappear. The disappearance is not total – there were always a few landscapes from earlier times without figures, and a few later ones with figures, but most landscapes up to the 1930s have figures and most post-1930s landscapes do not…

"What has become of the figures? It is easy to observe both amateur and professional photographers at work in Kings Park. They wait until any passing pedestrians are out of the way before the shoot. Moreover, people who see that a photograph [is] about to be taken step back and keep out of the field of view. And they know they don't belong. The only exception is when a "we were there" photograph is being taken… People in the foreground are a distraction because they particularise too strongly — we see their dress, which indicates the fashions of the year, even the season; and their bearing, which places them socially and economically. Perhaps television and the cult of the personality have wrought this change, and made people too individually specific in the detail of their appearance."

This is the end of the study, but the author added a postscript: "This essay in inconclusive. It asks a question and finds no answer. I still don't know the answer, and I still find the question interesting." I enjoy his honesty.

At about the same time, the English writer Adam Nicolson railed about the English disease of the "Pastoral", which in his opinion was a deluded ideal that shaped too many thoughts and practices: "…picture-England becomes an escape into the undemanding familiar, to places which you can consider yours in some vague and undefined way, and where you have rights but no responsibilities, a limited sort of freedom and no anxiety. It is for that reason that people almost never appear in picture-England. People make demands and will not always co-operate. People are difficult: picture-England never can be. This is a change in the last fifty years or so. 'Country characters' — the stand-by of *Picture Post* articles, or country writing before the war — rarely feature nowadays. Photographed England now looks as if a neutron bomb has hit it: no damage to buildings or landscapes but people have utterly been removed."

So people were being banished from the landscape, the same trend starting at about the same time, identified from two different areas of the globe. Even now, people are still missing. Weekend supplements of British newspapers often included directions for countryside walks. There was a photo of the area, usually with the sun shining, possibly with dramatic (but not threatening) clouds in the sky. Sheep and cattle might be seen, but no people. For about a year I collected these pages, and only once was a solitary figure shown, and then in the far distance. Perhaps the idea was to present the route as "one for you, so that you can commune with nature in splendid isolation". Calendars follow the same pattern. Look at any based on landscapes and try to find people. This is not limited to Great Britain, as over the years I have received annual offerings from both Switzerland and North America. All show stunning scenes, sometimes with buildings as well, but people are almost always missing.

Perhaps the most extreme example I have found of an image without people is a postcard – *Le Parc des Sources, Vichy. September 1969*. The card shows two lines of trees, standing in mown grass, with a path and hedge beside them. Little is shown of the crowns of the trees, and I can't even see the leaf shape clearly enough to identify the species. The shadows cast by the trees – rectangular shapes linking trunk to trunk – indicate that the crowns have been trimmed into shape following a formal, severely disciplined pattern, probably following the process called "curtain pruning". No one can be seen. The photograph is a patterned image, taken at the precise moment that the shadows link tree to tree across the grass.

Two centuries come together – a landscape that was executed in the 19th century but photographed by David Hockney in the 20th. The process that resulted in the photograph would have started even before planting. After the initial landscape design the specimens of the selected species would have been examined in the nursery and the best shaped examples chosen, before planting in precise positions. Then followed maintenance – especially pruning – that would have had to be meticulously executed over many years.

To me, the image caught by Hockney is remarkably clever, capturing with split-second timing the shadow pattern thrown by the pruned trees. However, there is a disparity. The materials of the landscape are natural – trees, grass, light – but they have been painstakingly manipulated by humans. Yet, despite this essential involvement, people have been banished from the photograph. Hockney later said he wanted "to photograph the unphotographable. Which is to say, space." On those grounds, perhaps their absence is inevitable.

Hockney's minimalist view is echoed by three other postcards that also avoid human presence. All show erratics, boulders transported by ice, carried in the vast sheets that covered much of the British Isles during the various ice ages. These examples are large enough to have remained where they grounded, probably cast aside by diminishing glaciers as temperatures slowly warmed and the ice retreated. The rocks appear out of place, stranded surprises, scoured and marked by their ancient journeys. To the west, the Burren on the Atlantic coast of Ireland; to the east, Whernside in the Yorkshire Dales; and north of these are rocks near the Cuillins in Skye.

All three cards follow the pattern that Seddon found in Australia and that which I have also seen in examples from Europe, North America and the United Kingdom. Scenes are chosen, often for their grandeur; very occasionally buildings are included, but people are omitted. From the images on these cards it is difficult to estimate the actual size of the boulders as there is nothing by which to scale them, but they are shown standing almost defiantly in isolated splendour.*

I have only one item in my collection that consciously includes people in the landscape, but even then the pictures could be classified as being in the "selfies/ we were there" category. From the mid-'40s to the early '60s, the Falkland Islands Dependencies Survey (later the British Antarctic Survey, but today's staff still refer to themselves as FIDS) looked after British interests in the Antarctic. I have only ten months of their 1959 calendar, but most of the landscape photos have men in them. Note – you can't always tell from the images that they are men, but this was the era before women were allowed to go South with the British. Figures are shown, skis over shoulder, or with a sledge and huskies, which were then permitted on the continent. Their backdrop happens to be a stunning landscape, but they wanted to be seen at work, heavily clad figures against snow-covered slopes.

So even though "landscape" is a concept discussed and debated by people, we often choose to eliminate them from images taken to show landscapes. Ansel Adams, the eminent American landscape photographer, was challenged about this and responded: "People have asked why I don't put people into my pictures of the natural scene. I respond, 'There are always two people in every picture: the photographer and the viewer'." That is true, but while we acknowledge that many landscapes, especially in the British Isles, are the results of human actions and influences, we still reject other people when we take photographs. I am guilty of this – my collection of slides and photographs have few people in them. When challenged, as I was after giving a lecture at an international conference, I was not able to give a coherent answer. Others have responded by suggesting that clothing

*An aside about postcards – they are disappearing. The days of holiday cards being sent to the family are gone. Apparently about two-thirds of interviewed holidaymakers said they had not sent postcards in the last ten years. Beyond blaming the mobile phone camera and the ease of the internet, examination of these trends is beyond my current thoughts, but I remember an episode when on holiday in Tenby, South Wales, and cards home were still expected. I made my choice from the revolving stand outside the ironmonger's shop (definitely not the usual sales point for cards) before going into the store to pay. Having seen my

would date the record, or awkwardness of posture would mar the image. I would add that I usually walk by myself and choose to avoid routes with many people, not from any dislike of the human race but because I find pleasure in such solitude.

The Scottish painter James Morrison spoke about his landscape works, usually executed out of doors. Speaking in the last years of his life, he said the views from his house "give rise to some terrific drama and show the independence of the landscape to man. That's deliberate. It's not that I've forgotten to put the people in. I don't want people in, and people seem a kind of irrelevance to what the landscape is doing, what the landscape is about." Like Ansel Adams, he was making a deeply considered statement, both in words and in paint.

Yet I have found occasions when human presence is seen as a positive benefit to enjoyment of the landscape. In an academic book about polar deserts, the respected biologist Professor William Benninghoff contributed a chapter in which he outlined the main biological and ecological features of those extreme landscapes. He closed his submission with a paragraph that presented ideas not found elsewhere in the polar literature of the mid-'70s. "Stepping still farther beyond my own speciality, I would hazard the opinion that we are ready to raise esthetic qualities of landscapes into our valuation lists. Polar landscapes in their natural states seldom fail to impress their beholder; therefore they have intrinsic esthetic value. This value might be expected to increase as the wilderness areas of lower latitudes undergo the continuing attrition and damage that show no signs of slackening. It is only fair to acknowledge, however, that often the human eye's delight in a wild landscape is heightened by a sign of harmonious human occupancy, a cabin, or a fishing boat, by people finding part of their sustenance in the land. We seem to have innate appreciation for the human presence in a compatible relationship with the landscape."

When I found his comments, I silently applauded his courage in raising the issue of aesthetic values, an issue that the polar community did not consider in any detail for another 20 years, but I was surprised at his suggestion of "innate appreciation for the human presence". I suspect my response was simply that I did not share his preference. But J. B. Jackson, American writer and publisher, did: "The older I grow and the longer I look at landscapes and seek to understand them, the

---

selection, the gentleman behind the counter smiled. I was curious and questioned his response. The answer came that I had conformed to the pattern he had observed over many years. If several cards were purchased, almost all customers had multiple copies of one favoured card, plus singles of one or two others. His was not a systematic, data-based survey, just an amusing but long-term observation. Over the years it has been thought-provoking – why was that the dominant pattern? I echo Seddon: "I still don't know the answer, and I still find the question interesting."

more convinced I am that their beauty is not simply an aspect but their very essence and that beauty derives from the human presence."

Both were writing about the same time, both expressed very similar ideas, both were Americans. Benninghoff was highly respected and published extensively, but mainly within his own academic field. Jackson was also widely published and, in addition, gave frequent lectures, so it is not impossible that they became aware of each other's views.

So there may well have been common ground between two thinkers from the same country, but the difference of understanding between nations should be recognised. An English academic offered the following, giving his own choice of emphases: "Values and traditions are clearly crucial to landscape meanings. American and English concepts of landscape are often assumed to be homogenous but the English view is closely tied in with *heritage* whereas the American perspective links more closely with *environment*; England has LANDSCAPE, the USA just landscape. Landscape values generally appear to focus on the past, rather than on potential landscape innovations." Every time I read his summary I smile. While I can on the whole agree with his heritage/environment assessment, I then come to his "LANDSCAPE/landscape" evaluation. I am still not certain if he was being provocative or whimsical or both.

Others have expressed pleasure in seeing animals in the landscape: Darwin's tiger on the plains or deer in the park – "how ones feelings would be excited, & how the scenery would rise" – but also the mountaineer Mallory. Writing about the approach of a climbing expedition to Everest in March 1924, Robert Macfarlane says Mallory surprised "a very fine jungle cat" in a glade, and wrote: "It is extraordinary how it makes the whole forest seem alive to see a beast like that." Mallory had been a history student at Cambridge, as was Darwin, 70 years earlier. Were Darwin's notebooks, now in the university library, accessible to him? Probably an unanswerable question and idle speculation, but it comes to mind before being gently put to one side.

For me, there is great joy in seeing a barn owl floating above a field in the dusk, or a skein of geese flying over my garden, but they do not colour my thoughts about the field or garden. What I have been able to observe will stay in my mind as a part of the whole rather than as a factor that "improves" the landscape. I prefer to remind myself that everywhere I go there is activity in the natural world, unseen but present, whether fungi beginning to break down leaves in the urban gutter, or fish swimming in the sea beside me as I walk along the beach.

Returning to the question that opened this chapter – can landscape ever be separated from people? "A Man in Assynt" is a poem by Norman MacCaig about the north-west Highland area, his mother's ancestral country.

Parts of the Scottish Highlands may have been less affected by human actions than other places in the British Isles, and neither legal ownership nor emotional attachment seem to influence the physical form of such a severe landscape. Yet MacCaig recognises his involvement – he sees himself as being possessed. Landscape is far more than just a physical entity so, in one way or another, people will always be there.

Who owns this landscape? —
The millionaire who bought it or
the poacher staggering downhill in the early morning
with a deer on his back?

Who possesses this landscape? —
The man who bought it or
I who am possessed by it?

False questions, for
this landscape is
masterless
and intractable in any terms
that are human.
It is docile only to the weather
and its indefatigable lieutenants —
wind, water and frost.

Views

A few years ago an article in *The Times* generated letters from parents about their efforts to interest their offspring in their surroundings. A father wrote about a visit to the Peak District when he attempted to get his daughters to put away their phones, enjoy nature and get fit. They then proceeded to "hike up to Kinder Scout at an impressive speed. My smug self-satisfaction at parental authority was short-lived. They were merely seeking a mobile signal." Another family, ascending a ski-lift, told the children to stop talking and look at the view. Their "ten-year-old withered me with a look and said, 'We are too young for views'".

Many parents will remember their own efforts to interest the family in various ways, but these exchanges raise questions about landscapes. What are "views"? Have views always been sought and enjoyed as they are today? If we are at a viewpoint, looking at the landscape before us, are we participating in the landscape or are we uninvolved spectators, standing on some sort of a sideline?

A delightfully simple but modern interpretation of a framed view can be seen at the National Botanic Garden of Wales. On the crest of a hill, overlooking the 1790s landscaped park, two natural timbers support a simple metal circle. The construction can be seen from a distance so as to attract visitors who walk up the gentle slope. The highlighted view follows the classic pattern of a middle-distance lake, surrounded by trees, with the water gently extending beyond immediate sight.

The author Robert Macfarlane presents some historical aspects: "There is scant evidence that any widespread aesthetic appreciation of views was in operation in Europe before the eighteenth century. Those who did find themselves at height among the mountains were often more concerned with the prospect of survival than with the prospect. The idea of the beautiful view, which now seems to us as instinctive a reaction to a landscape as is possible, does not seem to have had currency in the common consciousness, or at least not to have been triggered by mountains. Quite the opposite, in fact: until well into the 1700s, travellers who had to cross the Alpine passes often chose to be blindfolded in order to prevent them being terrified by the appearance of the peaks."

There are earlier examples of individuals who appreciated a specific view. In 1336 the Italian scholar Petrarch climbed Mount Ventoux in southern France. When on the mountain he read from Augustine: "Men go out and gaze in astonishment at high mountains, the huge waves of the sea, the broad reaches of rivers, the ocean that

Framing the landscape: sculpture by Rawleigh Clay, National Botanic Garden of Wales

encircle the world, or the stars in their courses. But they pay no attention to themselves." Petrarch is said to have understood this as an admonishment not to take joy in creation, but rather an injunction for men to be only concerned about their own salvation. I am sad he came to that conclusion – it is a limited interpretation of Augustine's thought as well as an unbalanced view of the Christian faith. Augustine held that if man was in a right relationship with God, the creation might be fully appreciated within that relationship. He was aware of the danger of simply seeing beauty but he recognised a true and valid response to the Creator: "The eyes delight in beautiful shapes of different sorts and bright and attractive colours. I would not have these things take possession of my soul. Let God possess it, he who made them all. He made them all *very good* [translator's footnote: Genesis 1 v31], but it is he who is my Good, not they."

In this country but about 350 year later, the naturalist John Ray wrote of his botanising expeditions on uplands, not only on the mild elevations of the South Downs, but on the higher, geologically layered slopes of Ingleborough in the Yorkshire Dales. He appreciated mountains and recognised them as "very ornamental to the Earth, affording pleasant and delightful Prospects, both 1. To them that look downwards from them upon the subjacent countries, as they must needs acknowledge who have been but on the Downs of Sussex, and enjoyed that ravishing Prospect of the Sea on one Hand, and the Country far and wide on the other. And, 2. To those that look upwards, and behold them from the Plains and low Grounds, which what a Refreshing and Pleasure it is to the Eye, they are best able to judge who have liv'd in the Isle of Ely, or other level Countries, extending on all Sides further than one can ken."

In thinking about mountains, Ray identified views looking down and views looking up. In relation to the latter, perhaps he was thinking of the Psalmist: "I lift up my eyes to the hills..." There are also views across, when the eye passes over intermediate sights, so as to focus on the distant.

Churchdown Hill is an outlier of the Cotswolds, a gently conical feature lying just over a couple of miles from the escarpment edge. The composer Herbert Howells spoke about the views from there: "I used to sit with Gerald Finzi and earlier still with Ivor Gurney on a hill halfway between Gloucester and Cheltenham and from there on a clear day... you could see the whole outline of the Malvern Hills 30 miles north... Gurney said to me one day, 'Look at that outline' – he meant the outline of the Malverns. He said: 'Unless that influences you for the whole of your life in tune

Near Churchdown, looking towards the Malvern Hills

making, or tune writing, it is failing in one of its chief essentials'. And of course outlines of hills and things are tremendously important if you have got a sense of line, if you are a composer. Of course you live according to your countryside. You can't help it ..."

"Living according to your countryside" describes the early years of Edward Wilson. Born in Cheltenham, he had the opportunity as a youth to roam the Cotswolds, especially the areas near Churchdown, investigating all aspects of natural history while perfecting his drawing and painting skills. His upbringing stood him in good stead during his later life in the Antarctic. His diary entry for 1 September 1891, when he was just 19, reads: "Dad gave me £5 and told me to go and walk in N Wales as long as the money lasted. Walked through Snowdonia and ascended Cader Idris."

In the Antarctic, among his many contributions to the expedition were panoramic views, detailed pencil drawings of distant coastlines or mountains. Often the features were many miles away, across the continent's ice plateau. Wilson could only observe from a distance, unable to visit. When surveying equipment was later used to locate and map features, his works were found to be accurate to a very precise degree. There are numerous comments by different members of the expedition about Wilson's contribution – he was clearly valued by all. In his journals Scott refers to the drawings as sketches, a description that somehow understates their worth. Their precision and skill elevates them beyond mere sketches.

About the same time as Scott and Wilson were in the Antarctic on their first visit, one specific English view was the subject of heated debate and formal action. In the summer of 1900 advertising boards appeared on the White Cliffs of Dover, just below the anti-Napoleonic fortification Western Heights. The Dover Corporation received a letter from the "Society for Checking the Abuses of Public Advertising" protesting at the erection of the hoardings, and the Councillors then requested the removal of the unlicensed advertising. Perhaps not surprisingly, they were ignored, so in August 1901 formal removal notices were issued which led to Quaker Oats Ltd applying retrospectively for a licence to retain them. This was refused, so in September another removal order was issued. Again, this was ignored, so the Council sent a formal notice of legal proceedings to commence in seven days. The hoardings were then quickly dismantled.

The website of the National Trust once stated: "The White Cliffs of Dover are perhaps most famous as an iconic landmark, the white chalk face a symbol of home and war time defence." The language has now been modified, but the sentiment frequently reoccurs. In this instance, many would think it a justifiable description of the cliffs. Was there also sensitivity that it was an American company that was advertising in this quintessentially British landscape?

At regular intervals the media explore the idea of the "best" landscapes or views in the British Isles, and I find their findings both interesting and educational. A structured survey was carried out by the *Daily Telegraph*, identifying "that Britons' sense of national identity depends far more on shared values and institutions than on nostalgia for warm beer and village cricket". Their findings were listed, with free speech leading the way. "The landscape of Britain" was fourth, the first tangible asset as opposed to a concept. *Country Life*'s contribution to the fray gave readers the opportunity to vote, and in this instance a view of Salisbury Cathedral over the water meadows triumphed.

One summer *The Sun* produced a wraparound cover with the proud proclamation: "This is our Britain." Forty-nine images were superimposed on a picture of idyllic countryside: "From The Angel of the North to the White Cliffs of Dover, with Mr Bean and the Loch Ness monster. This is what makes Britain great." It would be easy to criticise the newspaper's choice of "sights, scenes and characters", or its graphics, as there is little regard for scale or the incongruity of relationships. A Routemaster bus dwarfs the Eden Project in Cornwall, and a village cricket team plays beside a massive Giant's Causeway, but the issue I find more interesting is that no mention is made of its chosen backdrop – the rural scene of distant hills, wooded hedgerows, meadows and cropped fields. Perhaps that was intended as the 50th item on its list.

I can't draw conclusions from any of the surveys or presentations. If photographs have been used there is the added complication of the viewpoint, the weather and all the other factors influencing the final image. Nevertheless, reading what is considered to be valued, or not valued, gives at least a glimpse of others' preferences.

If a view or a specific landscape is described as "iconic", or even just "high quality", it is almost inevitable some will disagree. The Giant's Causeway is often praised, but Boswell records that the respected Dr Johnson commented that it was "worth seeing,

Quaker Oats advertisement hoarding 1900-1901, Dover, Kent

yes; but not worth going to see". It might be said that another area is far better, or there is a reaction against making comparisons, the whole concept of giving gradations such as poor, good or outstanding. As a young man, Wordsworth spent three months walking more than 2,000 miles in France and Switzerland. Thirty years later he retraced his steps, and when his *Guide to the Lakes* was republished under his name in 1822, he included comments about the Swiss landscapes. But he warned: "Nothing is more injurious to genuine feeling than the practice of hastily and ungraciously depreciating the face of one country by comparing it with that of another." He described Alpine landscapes but suggested that the viewer of the English Lakes, though not seeing the larger scale of the continental mountains, might make "the most of present objects" as "it is upon the mind which a Traveller brings along with him that his acquisitions whether of pleasure or profit, must principally depend". Echoes of Epictetus.

Wordsworth's enthusiasm for the high peaks and hills did not extend to all his friends. Charles Lamb wrote to him in January 1801: "I ought before this to have replied to your very kind invitation into Cumberland. With you and your sister I could gang anywhere; but I am afraid whether I shall ever be able to afford so desperate a journey. Separate from the pleasure of your company, I don't much care if I never see a mountain in my life. I have passed all my days in London, until I have formed as many and intense local attachments as any of you mountaineers can have done with dead nature." He goes on to list the joys of the capital: "The bustle and wickedness round about Covent Garden... the impossibility of being dull in Fleet Street; the crowds, the very dirt and mud, the sun shining upon houses and pavements... coffee-houses, steams of soups from kitchens; the pantomimes, London itself a pantomime and a masquerade – all these things work themselves into my mind, and feed me without a power of satiating me... So fading upon me, from disuse, have been the beauties of Nature, as they have been confidently called; so ever fresh and green and warm are all the inventions of men and assemblies of men in this great city."

An opposite response to the Lake District, written with vigour and good humour. Surely Lamb knew the response it would engender in his friend – affront at a phrase such as "dead nature" but knowing it was penned within the bond of a long-standing friendship.

Not many years later, but thousands of miles away in the southern hemisphere, Charles Darwin wrote notes about scenery in the extensive records he kept throughout the voyage in HMS *Beagle*. He saw no difficulty in making comparisons: "The pleasure derived from beholding the scenery and general aspect of the various countries we have visited, has decidedly been the most constant and highest source of enjoyment. It is probable that the picturesque beauty of many parts of Europe far exceeds anything we have beheld. But there is a growing pleasure in comparing the character of scenery in different countries, which to a certain degree is distinct from merely admiring their beauty. It more depends on an acquaintance with the individual parts of each view: I am strongly induced to believe that as in Music, the person who understands every note will, if he also has true taste, more thoroughly enjoy the whole."

Darwin showed a remarkable sensitivity when he suggested that "character" is different from "beauty". This is one of the fundamental concepts that underlies current thinking about landscape assessment. The basic principle is that every area has character, distinctive patterns that can be identified. Whether such patterns are "beautiful" is another matter, something that can follow once character has been established.

But there is a further approach, more subtle and perhaps more comfortable when considering the whole subject of landscape. The erudite cleric, artist and writer the Reverend William Gilpin visited many parts of Britain, introducing the "picturesque" as an aesthetic ideal. It was a time when travel for pleasure was beginning, and his pen and wash drawings of the landscapes stimulated interest. He linked beauty with what "is agreeable in a picture", and wrote that his prints were intended to "*characterize the countries* through which the reader is carried. The ideas are taken from the *general face of the country*; not from any *particular scene*." To me this is far more congenial, a gentler and more relaxed way to see landscape. Isolating and lauding a single view raises expectations that might not be met, but absorbing the whole rather than a specific part provides an overall and more rounded experience.

I found this approach in respect of a small item, perhaps more abundant in past years than now, but still part of our everyday life. David Gentleman designed more than a hundred stamps for the United Kingdom, and summarised their status when he wrote: "Stamps might seem too small to bother much about, but despite their scale, they are not insignificant. They are tempting to collect... They are also useful, even vital... This usefulness is precious, for it gives stamps a purpose and a validity... They are meant to be beautiful, serious, popular and profitable."

Probably his greatest contribution came in 1965 when Tony Benn, then Postmaster

General, commissioned him to write "Essays in Stamp Design", an album of experimental, non-traditional stamp designs. Gentleman listed topics that could be used for postage stamps, and included "characteristic regional landscapes (NOT specific beauty spots)".

He illustrated this with a page showing generic landscapes rather than precise views. The following year a set of four "Landscapes" was issued, with one stamp for each of the nations in the United Kingdom. While a specific feature (Harlech Castle) was illustrated for Wales, the other three stamps showed typical images, covering Sussex, Antrim and the Cairngorm Mountains. Many of the other suggestions he made in what became known as "The Gentleman Album" were taken up later.

I have not heard many adverse comments about views, only occasional gibes belittling those who visit outlooks so as to see panoramas. With growing age I suspect I am becoming more sensitive to such needs. I remember, for instance, the occasion when a trio of elderly relations with restricted mobility appreciated "the view" of a beach and the sea, presented to them from inside a car. It was early October and a warm spell, so the most agile of the group even went so far as to venture on to the sands and paddle in the gentle shallows. Climbing a dune would have been beyond her, but relatively easy steps enabled her to access the beach. Within reason, such provision should be made. I would not go as far as an American activist who developed an "access philosophy" that advocated, among other things, the construction of cable cars descending into the depths of the Grand Canyon. I am happy to know there are places that are beyond my walking or climbing capabilities, but within the scope of others. I prefer to congratulate them on their skills or abilities, knowing that their reward will be the sight and experience of such places.

Coming far closer to home, there is the case of the double sunset seen from the churchyard of Leek in Staffordshire. The sun drops below a hill to the north-west, then partially reappears from behind the steep northern slope before setting on the horizon. For the journalist Paul Simons, writing in *The Times*, a daily minute or two viewing this phenomenon, weather permitting, has been "spoilt" by trees. Apparently the phenomenon can still be seen from viewpoints near Leek and also in neighbouring Derbyshire, so observation of this curious pattern has not been completely lost. Others might argue that the sight of trees during daylight hours gives far more pleasure. I have not yet visited the churchyard so do not presume to judge. An interesting conundrum.

Imagined landscapes

I have been to the Natural History Museum only two or three times. Perhaps I should have found more opportunities to visit, but one item from that South Kensington palace of wonder has held my attention and given me pleasure for many years. It is a postcard of so-called "Landscape marble", more properly described as a polished slab of Rhaetian limestone cut from a quarry near Bristol. The photograph of a piece of rock, probably about 10cm by 5cm, suggests to me a group of trees towering above a hedge that borders a cultivated field, the lines of the plough or harrow running parallel to the boundary. The image brings to mind the English elms that used to be seen in the meadows near the Thames, or in arable lands across the Midlands. Sadly, the elms

"Landscape marble" – a polished slab of Rhaetian limestone from Cotham, Gloucestershire

were almost completely wiped out in the 1970s due to Dutch elm disease, but I still picture those landscapes in my mind.

My imagination has been stirred by a postcard. The reality is a piece of paper, but it displays an image of a piece of patterned stone and that in turn encourages my mind to remember past landscapes that have disappeared. Perhaps in time that particular configuration of trees and hedges will return, but for the moment it is only a memory. Other forms of expression have also been used to convey unseen landscapes. I have heard words describing regions of land and ice in such a way as to enable me to envisage them, yet the speaker had never seen the area for themselves. Others have encouraged and stirred my mind to reach out for reality, whether by written word, drawn image or speech.

Samuel Taylor Coleridge wrote "The Rime of the Ancient Mariner" without having seen Antarctic ice. It has been suggested he read Captain Cook's account of the first known crossing of the Antarctic Circle in 1773, or possibly the exploits of Captain Thomas James in the Arctic in the 1630s. Whichever explorer was his source, in a mere 12 lines Coleridge captures the feelings of ice of the Southern Ocean, the miserable coldness and the awe of ice and icebergs:

...And now there came both mist and snow,
And it grew wondrous cold:
And ice, mast-high, came floating by,
As green as emerald.

And through the drifts the snowy clifts
Did send a dismal sheen:
Nor shapes of men nor beasts we ken-
The ice was all between.

The ice was here, the ice was there,
The ice was all around:
It cracked and growled, and roared and howled,
Like noises in a swound!...

Later in his life, Coleridge wrote: "Poetry which excites us to artificial feelings makes us callous to real ones." In reading his verse, my feelings are definitely tinged with excitement, and bring to mind my own experiences of being in a ship heading south to the realms of ice. Coleridge had the ability to convey reality, despite his lack of personal experience.

Fifty years after Coleridge, the author Wilkie Collins wrote *The Frozen Deep*, a play possibly inspired by a recent report of Sir John Franklin's tragic expedition to the Arctic. The first performances had the author as one of the heroes and Charles Dickens as the other. By the standards of Victorian melodrama the play was perhaps no worse than many others; at the time it created something of a sensation, probably due to Dickens' acting ability, and a Command Performance was given in the presence of Queen Victoria and the Prince Consort. In her journal for 4 July 1857, Queen Victoria wrote: "An admirable Melodrama in 3 acts, by Wilkie Collins… most interesting, intensely dramatic, and most touching and moving at the end." *The Illustrated London News* of 17 January 1857 contained a wood engraving of the scenery for the third act, showing a cave with the sea behind where the rescue ship to the expedition stands at anchor. The most notable aspect of the play was the influence it appears to have had on Dickens. In his preface to *A Tale of Two Cities* (1859) he says he "first conceived the main idea of the story" when he was acting in *The Frozen Deep*.

I was involved with building work on a Victorian church, and during the renovations a double-page spread from the *Daily Telegraph* was found under the floor of the organ loft. Dated Tuesday, 4 January 1876, it included a fascinating "small-ads" page, giving details of items such as aluminium watches, billiard tables and Cupid's Magic Cards. Amidst numerous theatrical notices there were three heralding a "Great attraction" at the Strand Theatre Royal, a "bouffonnerie musicale" entitled *Antarctic, or the Pole and the Traces* by H. B. Farnie. "Beautifully new scenery" was promised, but how could an unknown continent be depicted and why was it the setting for a musical comedy? I pursued this oddity and ended up at the British Library reading the libretto. I found it made only passing reference to the continent. There were no directions regarding scenery, and I have not been able to find any descriptions or illustrations. Perhaps Farnie had been prompted to write it after Dickens' success with *The Frozen Deep*, or the departure in 1875 of a

British expedition to the North Pole, led by Captain George Nares. Whatever the stimulus, total ignorance of the landscape was clearly no impediment to production of a theatrical performance bearing its name. Mariners, a romantic couple, servants, schoolgirls and private detectives created an increasingly complicated situation, with many misunderstandings, but in the end all was resolved, leaving everyone to live happily ever after.

The polar regions are not the only zones of the world that have stirred the imagination of writers. About 50 years later than Coleridge's poem, the opening paragraph of Charles Kingsley's book *Hypatia* described a desert in Egypt, setting the scene for his historical novel about a 5th-century monk. Throughout the book occasional phrases continue to provide colourful and convincing accounts of arid desert, although Kingsley had never experienced such landscapes. Described as being capable of "brilliantly evocative descriptive passages", he also wrote of Central and South America, thus spanning the globe in his writing even though his own travels had been limited. John Buchan said his *Salute to Adventurers* was "the fruit of my enthusiasm for American history. In that book I described places in Virginia which I had never seen, and I was amazed, when I visited them later, to find how accurate had been my guesses." Buchan was not yet 40 when he wrote the book. Perhaps relative youth gave him the boldness to undertake such an enterprise.

Thomas Hardy wrote *The Woodlanders* in 1887, but in later editions added prefaces. In the second of these dating from 1912 he writes: "I have been honoured by so many enquiries for the true name and exact location of the hamlet 'Little Hintock', in which the greater part of the action of this story goes on, that I may as well confess here once and for all that I do not know myself where that hamlet is... To oblige readers I once spent several hours on a bicycle with a friend in a serious attempt to discover the real spot; but the search ended in failure; though the tourists assure me positively that they have found it without trouble, and that it answers in every particular to the description given in this volume."

Hardy loved "Wessex", an area extending across Wiltshire and Dorset, a real region that for him became an imagined place. In setting his stories he wrote sensitive descriptive passages, and as the popularity of his novels increased so did the number of visitors. Their certainty as to the location of the hamlet led Hardy to look for his imagined landscapes – a fruitless search despite the convictions of his readers. This seems to be the landscape equivalent of a kitten chasing its tail, an ineffective effort, but based on reality, providing a diversion from wider matters.

Occasionally artists have also imagined landscapes so as to convey them to others. Leeds City Art Gallery held an exhibition entitled "Points of vision" in which eight participants from different sections of a large legal firm in the city chose works from the gallery's collection loosely related to "landscape". One selection was Henry Moore's *Nine Imagined Views of Norway 1923*. A planned trip to the Scandinavian country fell through, but in writing to a friend to tell her of the cancellation Moore included a page of nine pen and ink miniature sketches. He listed them as: "1-4 A fiord, 5 Descent of fiord, 6 Glacier thawing, 7 Norwegian village, 8 Myself 1000 ft up, 9 Just to fill up the page [a landscape with a pond in the foreground and trees on the skyline]." On page 2 of his letter Moore wrote: "Norway is wonderful according to the Guide Book and what I remember of my school geography – (Page 1 is composed of scribbles of what I remember of the latter)."

The person who chose the Moore letter wrote a caption:

"I thought it was interesting to include in our exhibition a landscape of a place that the artist had never been. On our introductory session to this project we were asked to discuss the meaning of landscape and what landscape meant to us. As part of this we soon realised that everyone had preconceived or stereotypical ideas about various landscapes they too had never seen, which had come about through various media: literature, word of mouth, television and film. This is what Moore is giving us here."

While I was researching Antarctic "wilderness and aesthetic values" I talked to many people about the landscapes of the continent. For some who had already visited I used a survey pattern that enabled them to choose locations before talking freely about them, with no leading questions or promptings from me. During one interview the individual named a location on the Peninsula, and spoke of it in similar terms to other places he had selected. Only later did it emerge that the participant had never visited or seen the location, even from the air. Because of his work as a map-maker, it was as real to him as somewhere he had visited – he "knew" it as a place and felt able to talk about it, comparing it with others.

During different eras, and in differing places in the world, people responded to landscapes they had never seen, and could only imagine. Coleridge, Kingsley, Hardy and Buchan wrote, Henry Moore drew, the survey participant described in words – all were attempting to convey their imagined landscape to others.

Outlooks

For what you see and hear depends a good deal on where you are standing: it also depends on what sort of person you are." C. S. Lewis, academic, author and lay theologian, writing in one of his Narnia books, may seem a long way from landscape, but for me this seemingly simple statement has echoes in many aspects of life – including landscape. Our viewpoints may be actual geographical spots, or something abstract such as our social or political outlooks. On occasions, we might choose to have selective hearing. If all these variants are combined with "what sort of person you are", the permutations are endless but intriguing and worthy of exploration.

Initially I was surprised when I realised I had accumulated several passages about landscape and war. Taking a realistic view of the human race, perhaps it was inevitable. In the distant past, war was predominantly fought on land and sea, though now the air seems increasingly important. Chronologically my collection began with the lyrical prose of Edward Thomas, published in 1909:

"The north wind makes walking weather, and the earth is stretched out below us and before us to be conquered. Just a little, perhaps, of the warrior's joy at seeing the enemy's fair land from the hill-top is mingled with the joy in the unfolding landscape. The ploughlands brighten over twenty miles of country, pale and dry, among dark woods and wooded hills; for the wind has crumbled the soil almost white, so that a sudden local sunlight will make one field seem actually of snow. The old road following a terrace of the hills curves under yews away from the flinty arable and the grey, dry desolation round the poultry-farmer's iron house, to the side of a rich valley of oak and ash and deepening pastures traversed by water in a glitter. The green fire of the larch woods is yellow at the crest. There and in oak and ash the missel thrush is an embodiment of the north wind, summing it up in the boldness of his form and singing, as a coat of arms sums up a history. Mounted on the plume of the top of the tall fir, and waving with it, he sings of adventure, and puts a spirit into those who pass under and adds a mile to their pace. The gorse is in flower.

"In the hedges the goose-grass has already set its ladders against the thorns, ladders that will soon have risen to the top of every hedge like scaling ladders of an infinite army. Down from tall yew and ash hang the abandoned ropes of last year's traveller's joy that had leapt that height – who has caught them in the leap? – but the new are on their way, and even the old show what can be done as they sway from the topmost branches. At sunset an immense and bountiful land lies at our feet and

Goose grass climbing a holly hedge, Norfolk

the wine-red sun is pouring out large cups of conquest. The undulating ploughland is warm in the red light, and it is broken up by some squares of old brown stubble and of misty young wheat, and lesser green squares full of bleating and tinkling sheep. Out of these fields the dense beech copses rise sheer. Beyond, in the west, are ridges of many woods in misty conflagration; in the south-west, the line of the Downs under the level white clouds of a spacious and luminous sky."

The earth is to be "conquered"; goose grass becomes "scaling ladders of an infinite army"; "warriors" and "coats of arms" mingle with the missel thrush and gorse. When Thomas writes "the wine-red sun is pouring out large cups of conquest" is he remembering Jeremiah in the Old Testament? The prophet was told to take to disobedient nations a cup full of the wine of God's wrath as punishment, the "grapes of wrath" as in the "Battle Hymn of the Republic".

Thomas's imagery came as a shock. Can landscape be conquered? Should we even have the thought? But there is the sadness brought about by knowledge, the fact that *The South Country* was published less than ten years before Thomas died in a hideous war set in a scarred and unheroic landscape.

That landscape and the violence of war can be fused is sadly apparent in both fiction and fact. Dorothy Sayers' imaginary aristocratic detective, Lord Peter Wimsey, having served in World War I, is given the words: "'Now, when a painter paints a portrait of anybody,' went on Wimsey, 'that person's face is never the same to him again. It's like – what shall I say? Well, it's like the way a gunner, say, looks at a landscape where he happens to be posted. He doesn't see it as a landscape. He doesn't see it as a thing of magic beauty, full of sweeping lines and lovely colour. He sees it as so much cover, so many landmarks to aim by, so many gun emplacements. And when the war is over and he goes back to it, he will still see it as cover and landmarks and gun-emplacements. It isn't a landscape any more. It's a war map.'"

The fictional Lord Peter's words could almost come from a military sketching manual. "For over 200 years the discipline of field sketching has been an important element in fieldcraft attracting professional artists (who were forced to learn a range of new technical skills) whilst giving artistically talented soldiers the opportunity to practise their hands in unusually demanding circumstances... The discipline of panoramic drawing would reduce any landscape, however picturesque, into a series of immutable co-ordinates and fixed datum points." Apparently the discipline was covered in a 1956 manual, and limited use was still being made in the 1990s. Satellite and drone reconnaissance now dominate, but Lord Peter's views were replicated by a very real journalist, reporting about British troops serving in Afghanistan. Doug Beattie wrote: "It may seem strange but there is much to admire in the landscape of Helmand – its vivid colours and stark shapes, the lush foliage of the green zone, the endless desert with its water courses and ridges, the mountains always visible in the distance. And everywhere run the tree lines and irrigation ditches, natural and man-made features that the soldier sees with a different eye to the civilian. They provide cover for a patrol against small arms fire and allow stealthy movement through hostile territory. Over the years of British involvement in Afghanistan the enemy has watched and learnt our tactics, see how we avoid tracks and spaces... They understand our view of the land and our use of it."

Reduced to basics, this is identifying another use of the land, perhaps not immediately obvious but demanding attention. Whether armed forces are in the Middle East, the Falkland Islands or on peacekeeping missions in Africa, they need training – skills need to be taught, and this requires land. In East Anglia, the requirement has resulted in STANTA, the Stanford Training Area, used by the Army for "conflict operational training", to quote from an MOD document. Public access is severely limited, so when there was an opportunity to visit I went. At the time we were instructed not to use any form of camera, so the visit was free of technical appliances, which came as a surprisingly welcome restriction. With no possibilities for photographs, full concentration could be given to the real landscape.

Probably most of the party had already seen glimpses of the area on television as it had been the setting for many episodes of *Dad's Army*. Captain Mainwaring* marching his men past a belt of Scots pines closed many broadcasts, and the image certainly encapsulates much of the landscape of Breckland. In real life, the heath, woodlands, forest plantations, lakes, marshes and river are used by troops as they practise live firing, exploding demolition charges, vehicle and helicopter training, parachute drops and numerous other manoeuvres. I saw mature parklands surrounding what had been large country houses; large areas of Breck with birch, Scots pine and thorn; forestry plantations; and cropped turf grazed by large flocks of sheep. The lakes were typical of Norfolk, with occasional pingoes, circular ponds formed by melting ice at the end of the last ice age. Frog Hill was a vantage point

*During my visit I remembered the occasion when the panellists of an erudite radio quiz were asked which organisation was based in St Aldhelm's Church Hall. After discussion, they proffered "the Bloomsbury Group". The correct answer was Captain Mainwaring and his platoon. I found it enjoyable that an imaginary, ramshackle crowd triumphed over such a talented and influential gathering.

A pingo on Thompson Common, Norfolk

Breckland on a late December afternoon:
the track is Peddars Way, with STANTA to the left

where, despite its low elevation, the inner core of the training area stretched into the distance, a vast (for Norfolk) extent of heather and grass which looked calm and gentle in the setting sun.

What we were seeing from that viewpoint in Breckland was a peaceful, almost idyllic, scene, "the landscape of a hundred years ago" as one visitor put it. But it was a sanitised and limited view, devoid of the activity that had been the prime factor in its moulding and development over the last 60 years. There were no machine guns firing live ammunition over our heads, no landing parachutes or artillery fire. The unsettling thought was the realisation that we were observers of, rather than participants in, the landscape. Unless we are farmers, we are often observers of the rural landscape, but there is usually a greater degree of involvement possible, as we walk along footpaths or use the opportunities given to us to roam. Here we were denied that freedom, and had to be content with being spectators from afar.

C. S. Lewis also included hearing in his observation, a sense often forgotten when thinking about landscape. It had been remembered by Thomas Hardy, writing a century or so before Lewis. The setting of *The Return of the Native* is Egdon Heath, Hardy's name for the Dorset heathlands. He writes vivid descriptions of the landscape, including a marvellous passage recognising the place of sound, the contribution it makes to the whole:

"The wind... seemed made for the scene, as the scene seemed made for the hour. Part of its tone was quite special; what was heard there could be heard nowhere else. Gusts in innumerable series followed each other from the north-west, and when each one of them raced past the sound of its progress resolved into three. Treble, tenor, and bass notes were to be found therein. The general ricochet of the whole over pits and prominences had the gravest picture of the chime. Next there could be heard the baritone buzz of a holly tree. Below these in force, above them in pitch, a dwindled voice strove hard at a husky tune, which was the peculiar local sound alluded to. Thinner and less immediately traceable than the other two, it was far more impressive than either. In it lay what may be called the linguistic peculiarity of the heath... being audible nowhere on earth off a heath.

"...It was a warm whisper, dry and papery, and it brushed so distinctly across the ear that, by the accustomed, the material minutiae in which it originated could be realized as by touch. It was the united products of infinitesimal vegetable causes, and these were neither stems, leaves, fruit, leaves, prickles, lichen, nor moss."

Hardy used musical terms in his descriptions of sounds in the landscape. When asked to compose music to accompany the 1948 film *Scott of the Antarctic*, Ralph Vaughan Williams had to consider how to use the forces available to him – the vast array of musical instruments, including the human voice – to convey sounds he could only imagine, or hear from the limited number of available sound recordings. His widow, Ursula Vaughan Williams, wrote that he revelled in the challenge of finding "musical equivalents for the physical sensations of ice, of wind blowing over the great, uninhabited desolation, of stubborn and impassable ridges of black and ice-covered rock, and to suggest man's endeavour to overcome the rigours of this bleak land and to match mortal spirit against elements". Vaughan Williams later augmented the film music and composed "Sinfonia antartica", generally seen as his seventh symphony.

Another writer who wrote about landscape convincingly was W. H. Hudson. Brought up on the pampas of Argentina, the son of American settlers, he came to England in his late twenties. He wandered the countryside, writing about what he experienced, and his work is seen as influential in the development of the "back to nature" movement of the 1920s and '30s. In his foreword to Hudson's *Afoot in England*, Robert Macfarlane described Hudson's practices of "letting the landscape lead him... waiting for happenstance and alignments to issue into revelation". This approach is illustrated by Hudson's account of his experiences as he neared an unnamed English town. It is still linking landscape and sound, but at the other end of the scale of audibility:

"In the course of a ramble on foot in a remote district I came to a small ancient town, set in a cuplike depression amidst high wood-grown hills. The woods were of oak in spring foliage, and against that vivid green I saw the many-gabled tiled roofs and tall chimneys of the old timbered houses, glowing red and warm brown in the brilliant sunshine – a scene of rare beauty, and yet it produced no shock of pleasure; never, in fact, had I looked on a lovely scene for the first time so unemotionally. It seemed to be no new scene, but an old familiar one; and that it had certain degrading associations which took away all delight.

"The reason of this was that a great railway company had long been 'booming' this romantic spot, and large photographs, plain and coloured, of the town and its quaint buildings had for years been staring at me in every station and every railway carriage which I had entered on that line. Photography degrades most things, especially open-air things; and in this case, not only had its poor presentments made the scene too familiar, but something of the degradation in the advertising pictures seemed to attach itself to the very scene. Yet even here, after some pleasureless days spent in vain endeavours to shake off these vulgar associations, I was to experience one of the sweetest surprises and delights of my life.

"The church of this village-like town is one of its chief attractions; it is a very old and stately building, and its perpendicular tower, nearly a hundred feet high, is one of the noblest in England. It has a magnificent peal of bells, and on a Sunday afternoon they were ringing, filling and flooding that hollow in the hills, seeming to make the houses and trees and the very earth to tremble with the glorious storm of sound. Walking past the church, I followed the streamlet that runs through the town and out by a cleft between the hills to a narrow marshy valley, on the other side of which are precipitous hills, clothed from base to summit in oak woods. As I walked through the cleft the musical roar of the bells followed, and was like a mighty current flowing through and over me; but as I came out the sound from behind ceased suddenly and was now in front, coming back from the hills before me. A sound, but not the same – not a mere echo; and yet an echo it was, the most wonderful I had ever heard. For now that great tempest of musical noise, composed of a multitude of clanging notes with long vibrations, overlapping and mingling and clashing together, seemed at the same time one and many – that tempest from the tower which had mysteriously ceased to be audible came back in strokes or notes distinct and separate and multiplied many times.

"The sound, the echo, was distributed over the whole face of the steep hill before me, and was changed in character, and it was as if everyone of those thousands of oak trees had a peal of bells in it, and that they were raining that far-up bright spiritual tree music down into the valley below. As I stood listening it seemed to me that I had never heard anything so beautiful, nor had any man – not the monk of Eynsham in that vision when he heard the Easter bells on the holy Saturday evening, and described the sound as 'a ringing of a marvellous sweetness, as if all the bells in the world, or whatsoever is of sounding, had been rung together at once'.

"Here, then, I had found and had become the possessor of something priceless, since in that moment of surprise and delight the mysterious beautiful sound, with the whole scene, had registered an impression which would outlast all others received at that place, where I had viewed all things with but languid interest. Had it not come as a complete surprise, the emotion experienced and the resultant mental image would not have been so vivid; as it is, I can mentally stand in that valley when I will, seeing that green-wooded hill in front of me and listen to that unearthly music."

It was inevitable that after reading this description I should try to pinpoint the town and the tower. As a bellringer, any description of bells, especially by non-ringers, attracts and interests me. I spent considerable time trawling through online images of railway posters of the era; I wrote to Robert Macfarlane; I edited Hudson's passage and used it as a basis for an article published in the weekly journal *The Ringing World*, and asked if ringers could recognise the church and its tower. I have yet to receive any answers, or even suggestions to be pursued. No source put forward a location that fitted Hudson's descriptions. Perhaps the passage was an amalgam, a blended picture Hudson composed from different places, but somehow this does not ring true to his life and other writings. Meanwhile, I shall continue reading Hudson with delight.

A few years ago I received a letter from a friend with whom I had worked for many years, who lived in a predominantly arable part of East Anglia. He wrote: "Autumn is here... and once again I am aware of the autumn sounds in the countryside – tractors ploughing and perhaps grain driers drying! Nostalgia – back to school – back to college – prospect of winter – melancholy.

"It occurs to me that not only are the sounds different because of the agricultural seasons but the echo-reverberation time of the landscape will differ greatly with the seasons as crop cover reverts to ploughed ground etc etc. (A further subtlety on top of the natural differences between valley/flatland acoustics and woodland/beach acoustics.) Is it 'naturally melancholic'?! If the ploughed ground is more sound reflective than the stubble, we probably hear more distant sounds immediately after ploughing? Also what about the weather – cloud cover versus clear sky etc? The town dweller misses these seasonal fluctuations."

Many questions and no immediate answers. Are we sufficiently aware of sound in our lives? As I write, two occasions relating to landscape come to mind. One linked to a path a few yards from my house; the other to a small hill, many thousands of miles away.

Beginning at home, the path is a route to the centre of town, a very narrow passage between houses that then runs beside a car park. A bank of shrubs separates cars from humans, and these bushes sometimes shelter a gathering of sparrows. Their vibrant chirps and cheeps, seemingly continuous conversations, are a raucous but welcome addition to the walk. One list of collective nouns suggests "a quarrel of sparrows", another "a host". Neither seems appropriate, at least to my group of those delightful birds. To me they are not quarrelling, but conversing in a disordered fashion, similar to a group of young children sitting round a school table, eating their lunch. None has yet learned the art of conversation – the discipline of "one at a time" or the pause to consider what has been said. I walk by the shrubs as silently as possible, intent on not disturbing the discussion.

The small hill was climbed during my first visit to Antarctica, observing a tourist cruise. The ship visited Paradise Harbour as at the time it was the location of an active Argentine research station "Almirante Brown". Small buildings hugged the shoreline and were partly shielded from northern winds by a rocky bluff. Cruise members were told that during the visit they could see round the station and, if they wished, go up the slope unaccompanied. Safety procedures usually dictated that we were escorted everywhere, with frequent head counts to ensure all were present. While the conducted station tour was taking place, I chose to go up the hill. It was one of the few opportunities there had been during our limited time on land to be alone in the landscape.

It was early summer in the Antarctic, and snow still lay on most of the land. The sea ice was broken but continued to cover much of the bay. I was able to be at the top of the hill by myself for about 20 minutes, enjoying the bright sun and spectacular view. Yet there was continuous noise. Diesel generators provided power to the station, an essential supply but producing an unremitting, relentless sound that permeated the whole landscape.

There were occasions when I experienced silence, but they were limited. During my second visit I was based at a research station on a peninsula, and we were allowed to walk alone in a limited way. There were occasions when it was warm enough to sit for a few minutes in a sheltered spot; and, depending on the direction of the wind, noises from the station might be lost. My Antarctic experience was very different from that of earlier visitors. In the 1930s a scientific worker wrote: "Herbert Ponting, Scott's photographer, had said that he could hear whales blowing five miles away in the still air of this very place [the Bay of Whales]. And I had always found this difficult to believe, like many of the stories Antarctic explorers tell, but as I stood there... on the great Ross Barrier in seventy-eight degrees south, I gave posthumous acknowledgement to Ponting that this expeditioner's tale at least was true and, indeed, I could better it for I heard distantly the sighing of the sea under the barrier cliff six or seven miles away." So noise in the Antarctic can be heard at great distances, probably more than would be considered normal in other parts of the world.

Therefore, my experience of sound in the landscape is mixed. At the most local level it is positive, the pleasure in hearing birds that are sadly declining in number. Even though it is more than 40 years since I sat on that hill in the Antarctic, I still remember the conflict – sadness at hearing the intrusive, man-made noise but knowing it was essential for continued life in an extremely hostile environment. Noise is often part of the human experience in Antarctica. In a tent there is the Primus, on the move the engine of the skidoo, at base the diesel generators. There are limited opportunities to escape the tyranny, so often part of our lives wherever we might be.

Paradise Harbour, Danco Coast, Antarctic Peninsula

Dhofar Mountains near Salalah, Oman

Wandering stone, Death Valley, California

Surprise landscapes

The author Robert Macfarlane recounts sailing in an open boat from the north of Lewis to Orkney: "The water gurgled and slapped, as if it had thickened. I thought of Pytheas, the Greek voyager who had sailed north from France in 325 BC, following established trade routes to begin with – the 'tin road', the 'amber road' – and then just kept going, pausing on Lewis to erect his gnomon and take readings of sun height and day length, before sailing still further north, until he reached a latitude where the sea turned gelid with the cold and the air palled with freezing mists, such that the atmosphere resembled what Pytheas enigmatically called a 'sea-lung' (*pneumon thalassios*)."

Pytheas experienced the gradual beginning of the freezing of the sea – the almost oily appearance of the surface, which is followed by the build-up of crystals in a myriad of forms that ultimately coalesce to create a solid surface. Andy Goldsworthy, land artist and photographer, was a more recent Arctic visitor who wrote: "I keep referring to the place as a 'landscape' – the landscape in which I work... When I was riding over the ice I thought, this isn't land, this is water, so is it a waterscape? But it is as solid as the earth, for the moment. The more I work with the snow and ice, the more I realise there is so much to learn... everything is fluid, even the land, it just flows at a very slow rate."

Even before Pytheas, and about two and a half thousand years before Goldsworthy, the phenomenon was described in the Old Testament book of Job:

> *From whose womb comes the ice?*
> *Who gives birth to the frosts from the heavens?*
> *when the waters become hard as stone,*
> *when the surface of the deep is frozen?*

There is much debate about the date of the Old Testament book of Job, but I am content with the suggestion that it was anonymously written some time during the period 600-400BC. Job had suffered catastrophic losses, and three friends offered him plodding and unsympathetic advice, leading Job to call them "miserable comforters". The vocabulary of the book has made translation extremely complex, leading Luther to complain about the difficulties he faced attempting to enable the patriarch Job to speak idiomatic German. Despite these problems, Luther described the book as "a giant because it contains profound teachings wrapped in beautiful dress".

The Lord responded to Job's situation, not by giving easy answers to the challenge of his sufferings, but by asking him questions centred around the created world. The Lord's words immediately illustrate Luther's "beautiful dress": morning stars sing; phrases such as "storehouses of the snow" or loosening "the cords of Orion" complement the flying hawk and the soaring eagle. But beyond these poetic and moving words lies a question. How could the writer have known about waters becoming "hard as stone"?

It is known that trading expeditions went to Northern Europe for commodities such as tin, flint and amber. Goods were brought south, either by sea-going ships or overland and by rivers, following the "Amber Road" that linked the Baltic to the Mediterranean. After such travels, tales must have been told of places visited and sights seen, giving people in the often hot, dry and sometimes barren Middle East a description of sea ice – a component of a landscape unknown to them. It is seemingly stable but always moving, apparently solid but ultimately liquid. These mysteries, seen in distant northern seas, may have been described to a few, but through the book of Job they were presented to many.

So two and a half thousand years ago the people in the Middle East were introduced to an unknown northern landscape. As one living in the 21st century with access to the internet and almost unlimited opportunities to travel (at least during pre-COVID times), I doubt if I can ever experience totally "unknown landscapes", but there can be "surprise landscapes".

I assumed the Arabian Peninsula to be a hot, sandy and mountainous desert, but a television programme about Dhofar in Oman showed tropical, deciduous forests, enabled to grow because monsoon winds hit an escarpment and drop rain.

A calendar showed two or three of the wandering stones in Death Valley in North America. It was only about 10 years ago that an explanation was given for at least some of the movement of these rocks. Water gathered on the desert lake bed and then froze; but when sun melted the surface, the movement of thin panes of ice pushed the rocks, leaving scour trails. Even with this explanation, these sailing stones exert an almost mystical fascination – mystical only in the sense of transcending my immediate understanding and leaving me with a sense of questioning wonder.

On the Antarctic Peninsula the 300-mile-long George VI Ice Sound separates Alexander Island from Palmer Land. At its southern end the Sound meets the English

Coast (named after an American member of the United States Antarctic Service, which surveyed the area in the 1940s), and the "chocolate bar" fracturing of the ice presents an immediately fascinating aerial image. Then follow thoughts about the extreme danger, if not impossibility, of surface travel by whatever means.

British Antarctic Survey Twin Otter flying over a crevassed icefield on the English Coast, Palmer Land

Nearer to home, and many years ago, I saw the hollies on Holmstone Beach, Dungeness. Thickets of holly, shaped by the wind, grow on shingle ridges. Their origin is unknown, but they are at least 400 years old. Public access is severely limited as the Army has used the area for training since 1881, and gravel extraction has also damaged or removed plants. I still remember my immediate thrill when I first saw them – my thought was that I was seeing a Japanese Zen garden writ large. My slide photograph may be old, but it still conveys the strangeness of the ancient forms.

Landscapes continue to surprise and generate free and joyful thoughts. Pytheas was remembered by Macfarlane, and reading that passage reminded me of Job, so within a few seconds two and a half thousand years and three thousand miles were mentally traversed, prompting images of the seas around the Scottish Isles, ice in polar seas and the arid Middle East. Links can span both time and space.

Moving even farther north, to the Arctic, I read about the visit to England of Anaviapik, a hunter-gatherer from the Inuit community at Pond Inlet on Baffin Island. As an elder of his community, he had been chosen to come to England to check the veracity of a film made about his land. It was the first time he had left the Canadian High Arctic, and his host, social anthropologist Hugh Brody, recounts Anaviapik's responses to different landscapes:

"Over the next two weeks, we often played the game of seeing if Anaviapik could guide us from Bayswater tube stop to my flat – a distance of about half a block, with one left turn, a crossing of the road and a climb of half a dozen steps to the building's front door. He never succeeded. He always expresses mock dismay at being lost and enjoyed reminding me that, since we lived in cliffs, of course our houses were not easy to tell one from the other... To get some relief from homogenised urban crowds, we took a trip to the Norfolk countryside. I wanted to give Anaviapik some sense of an England that is not all cliffs and cliff dwellers. We set off, driving northeast, across Cambridgeshire and through Suffolk. I chose a route that was as rural as could be. He looked out onto the green landscape and said, "It's all built". He did not see the difference between town and country except as a matter of degree: the one had more people and houses side by side, and the other had more fields and hedgerows. But all of this, hedgerows as much as houses, was made by people; none of it was 'nature' – at least, not a form of nature that he would recognise as such. He was always amiable and interested, but he did not like much of what he saw."

Anaviapik's response to the English agricultural landscapes may have been a surprise to his companion, but from a historical point of view it was remarkably accurate. Whatever routes were taken, the countryside between London and Norfolk has been formed by man – so in Anaviapik's terms it was not "natural". This response appears to have come as a surprise to Brody, but he later understands the Inuit's response and writes: "Where agriculture has no place, beyond the farmer's frontier,

Holmstone hollies, Kent

there is no such thing as countryside. Instead, there is wild, raw nature, a wilderness." Countryside and wilderness may both be described by the single word "landscapes", but wilderness can never be described as countryside.

Brody had studied and worked with the Inuit during the 1970s. The Austrian-born American designer Victor Papanek lived with Alaskan Inuit 30 years earlier, and wrote of the skills that enabled them to live in such severe conditions. He suggested that their acute powers of observation and a highly retentive memory played a critical part in their existence. Papanek noted that when travelling through unfamiliar country his companion would be continually glancing backwards so as to become familiar with the route they would take on their return journey. "Inuit use natural signifiers... contextual relationships. These relationships will include wind, salinity of the air, slight contour changes, type and moisture and hardness of snow, moisture content of the air, distance to shore... The orientation of Inuit... is a necessity for survival honed to perfection by a lifetime of experience. It has to do with abstracting essentials from landscape and climate... A hunter will notice even the slightest change in the wind from the direction in which the fur on his parka blows: an organic sextant."

I was fascinated by two illustrations that accompanied Papanek's descriptions. A map of a coastal area drawn from memory by an Inuit hunter was compared with one generated by modern techniques. The similarities of the scattered islands, together with the indentations of bays and creeks, were amazing. Even more interesting was the photograph of two carved wooden objects, intricate pieces of wood, apparently carefully fashioned but with irregular and seemingly haphazard edges. Shown without an explanation, few could fathom their purpose. The caption below these driftwood artefacts read: "Inuit carved wooden maps from Greenland were made to be read by the fingers. They are waterproof, and will float if dropped overboard." Properties not endowed to a mobile phone, or a paper map, however well encapsulated. They were offered for sale by an Inuit from Eastern Greenland in 1885, before finding their way to Denmark, and then being repatriated to Greenland.

However, the understanding given by Papanek to these items is not accurate. Hans Harmsen, the deputy director of the Greenland National Museum, has written: "...woodcarving was a common activity among the Tunumiit... The Inuit people have used carvings in a certain way – to accompany stories and illustrate important information about people, places, and things. A wooden relief map would have functioned as a storytelling device, like a drawing in the sand or snow, that could be discarded after the story was told... in Inuit tradition, the act of making a map was frequently much more important than the finished map itself. The real map always exists in one's head. Though the maps themselves are unique, the sentiments and view of the world they represent were universal to the culture that made them... There is, in fact, no ethnographic or historical evidence that carved wooden maps were ever used by any Inuit peoples for navigation in open water, and there are no other similar wooden maps like these found in any collection of Inuit material anywhere else in the world."

So two simple pieces of wood conveyed knowledge held in the maker's mind to others with less understanding of the terrain. Their carefully shaped forms expressed

*Inuit wooden "maps"
of the East Greenland
coast, c1885*

an understanding of the landscape, far beyond the capabilities of most others experiencing that land.

Papanek also made a comment that could give an understanding to Anaviapik's inability to find his way in an urban area. Papanek suggests that both the summer tents of skin or hide and the winter igloo are dome-shaped with no vertical or parallel planes, no right angles or straight lines. "Until the 1960s Western notions of rectangular enclosed space were still fairly unfamiliar to most Inuit... The igloo creates an omni-directional space from which the Western concepts of linear or hierarchical order, sequence and series are curiously absent." This radically different orientation system, apparently still current in the 1950s and '60s, would have been present in Anaviapik's childhood, and would perhaps have been influential in his response to the linear and angular environment of London streets. With the changes in the patterns of life in many, if not most, parts of the world, it has to be questioned whether a 21st-century Inuit would have the same difficulties.

C. S. Lewis also explored concepts behind words that gave the setting for human activities, reinforcing the need for awareness of context, for whatever reason – geographical, cultural or political. "Where towns are few and very small and where nearly everyone is on the land one is not aware of any special thing called 'the country'... 'the country' is simply the world, what water is to a fish." He suggests that the writers of the Psalms "naturally give us little landscape. What they do give us, far more sensuously and delightfully than anything I have ever seen in Greek, is the very feel of weather – weather seen with a real countryman's eyes... Everyone was close to the land; everyone vividly aware of our dependence on soils and weather. To say that God created Nature, while it brings God and Nature into relation, also separates them. What makes and what is made must be two, not one. Thus the doctrine of creation in one sense empties Nature of divinity... [and] makes her an index, a symbol, a manifestation, of the Divine."

Lewis highlights Psalm 104* where alternating passages look objectively at God as Creator with sections that joy in the creation. A simple list, in order of occurrence, from that one Psalm, reads: light, water, clouds, wind, fire and flames, the deep, mountains, thunder, valleys, springs, river-valleys, fields, animals (including wild donkeys, goats, rock-badgers, and lions in their prime), birds, crags, moon, sun, night, forest, foliage, grass, greenery, trees (especially the cedars of Lebanon and fir trees), moon, forests, and the sea, with "Leviathan, which you formed to frolic there".

*In passing, verses 15 and 16 of this Psalm mention "bread from the earth, wine that gladdens human hearts...and bread that sustains their hearts". Another theologian, belonging to a church in which many members were teetotallers, once murmured to me: "I am glad that verse is in the Bible."

So no "landscape", no "scenery", no "environment", but a vibrant and caring description of the writer's surroundings, filled with joy, respect and praise to the Lord of Creation.

An oddity that defies precise classification – a journalist in *The Times* mentioned a leaflet for tourists, describing Yorkshire coastal communities in Holderness that had been destroyed by the encroaching North Sea. A local resident was quoted: "Essentially what you're doing is looking at what's not there. That's part of the irony of it." Not at all comical to those on the east coast who are still losing their properties, but surely there is something incongruous and tending towards dark humour in following a trail of invisible sites.

Landscape does not frequently generate outright laughter. The nearest I have come to that was my surprise on seeing a hillside in Northern Ireland. While I am not generally in favour of graffiti, especially in rural areas, I admit the slogan painted on rocks near Castlewellan in support of the local Gaelic sports team made me laugh. A knowledge of the six counties of the North is necessary, but the simplicity of the two-word message is commendable: "UP DOWN".

Single words

Understanding "landscape" in my own language continues to be an ongoing process. The stamp showing the scientists and their jigsaw puzzle will always be in my mind. They had completed a small section but the whole was still unaccomplished. I suspect this will be the case for me and landscape.

At school I learnt French and German and later taught myself elementary New Testament Greek, but I am not a confident linguist. I might be able to ask for directions or order a meal, but I cannot communicate in depth or understand any subtleties of speech. I value opportunities to speak with others, but if there is a language barrier I feel a great loss. I look back and can remember pleasurable and sometimes lengthy conversations, sometimes with farmers or their wives, or the couple who stopped by the gate of our holiday cottage, or the postmistress who took 20 minutes to sell me a few stamps. English was our common tongue, and despite other differences we were able to speak with understanding of each other and go a little way beyond initial courtesies and exchange of factual information.

So to read about complexities relating to understanding the single word "landscape" in another language is daunting. I had a brief visit to Japan when our daughter was studying there. We travelled by public transport, seeing southern parts of the country, including some of the outlying islands. I was able to look and enjoy with my Western-orientated eyes, but had no sensitivity to any linguistic subtleties. A couple of years after my visit I read about two academic researchers who found there are three terms that indicate "landscape" in Japanese. In the end, they could focus on only two of them, *fukei* and *keikan*, as they encountered severe difficulties in finding a consistent description of the concepts suggested by the third, *keshiki*.

For a start, I find it disconcerting that a word cannot be even vaguely defined. I recognise that their study was small, but the interviewees, asked to define the words, and distinguish between them, came from a range of areas – urban, suburban and rural – so that aspect of the research was as good as it could be. It is unsettling to put aside a word because it is so flexible or vague. What are its origins? Why does it exist? Can it ever be used, if there is not going to be at least a modicum of common ground between the speaker and the hearers?

With respect to the other two terms, the research results indicated that the two refer to distinctive concepts or representations of landscape that may not be taken as equivalent. *Fukei* refers to a traditional or cultural Japanese landscape, dominated by elements such as mountains, rice fields, trees, flowers and villages as well as shrines and temples and sacred natural elements. Its meaning was summed up as "the typical landscape of Japan". Interestingly, all interviewees also mentioned acoustic associations, such as the sounds of animals and birds. *Keikan* is connected with a visual impression of the landscape, and generally is seen as a modern, artificial term covering cityscapes and even fictitious or virtual landscapes.

That formal research illustrated difficulties found in just one language, and left me wondering how many other languages had similar subtleties. Then a brief note in a newspaper mentioned a Welsh word, *cynefin*, which the journalist suggested meant "heartlands… one's biological, cultural, geographic and spiritual habitat". My small Welsh dictionary translates the noun as "haunt, habitat" and the linked adjective as "acquainted, accustomed, familiar". Not exactly "landscape" but a close cousin in the family of thoughts.

I drafted these thoughts about *cynefin* one afternoon, and that evening came across another Welsh word, *hiraeth*. It is "a Welsh word for which there isn't really an English equivalent. It conveys within its meaning a deep longing, especially for one's home. This is the feeling many Welsh people have for their home country, a longing to experience 'the green, green grass of home' once again." Coincidence to be considering the two words on the same day, but another indication of the intensity of emotion that can be generated by landscape, especially that of home.

The first trio of words

Twice in my life I have been presented with a three-word phrase that has had implications far beyond the simplicity of their immediate or obvious meaning. A different trio each time, and separated by about 30 years, but on both occasions just three simple words have resulted in me being pushed to explore ideas far beyond the comfort zone in which I was then living. I had to read, think and probe, before coming to some sort of understanding. Even then, the issues each trio raised have been ongoing and have demanded continued thought and exploration, with conclusions that will not be static or forever fixed and unassailable.

The first trio was presented to me at college, when studying landscape architecture in the mid-1960s. There was growing international recognition of environmental issues, and an American historian, Lynn White Jr., contributed to the debate. In 1967 the reputable and widely read journal *Science* published his paper, "The historical roots of our ecological crisis". The bone of contention offered by White and subsequently by many others, is remarkably small, just the three words: "multiply and subdue". They are taken from the King James version of the Bible, the first chapter of the book of Genesis, and form part of the creation mandate given by God to humans.

Taken from their context and supported by examples of undeniably tragic misuse of resources in the Western world, the command to "multiply and subdue" was used to place the blame for environmental degradation and disasters on the Judeo-Christian tradition. White's approach was taken up by Ian McHarg, a landscape architect of Scottish birth who worked mainly in the United States. He wrote an influential book, *Design with Nature*, published originally in 1969 but currently running into its 25th edition, a clear indication of popularity. It has been, and probably will continue to be, very influential in the work of environmentalists, whether planners, ecologists, landscape architects or any other of the linked disciplines.

White's views hit me hard because, as a relatively recently convinced Christian, I held the Bible as the inspired word of God, his way of telling us about himself and the way we should lead our lives. I studied all 66 books, reading historical narratives, passages of poetry and prophecy, densely packed theological arguments, practical advice to struggling individuals or churches and, most importantly, accounts of the life of Jesus. Were the attacks on this phrase justified, and what was my response?

White's and McHarg's views about "multiply and subdue" were both supported and challenged by others in the environmental community. It was pointed out that their case was limited to an attack on a single chapter, before taking a selective part of a single verse in that chapter. There was a simplification of Genesis 1, verses 26 and 27, which read in full: "So God created man in his own image, in the image of God created he him; male and female created he them. And God blessed them, and God said unto them, Be fruitful, and multiply, and replenish the earth, and subdue it: and have dominion over the fish of the sea, and over the fowl of the air, and over every living thing that moveth upon the earth."

The injunction to replenish the earth was almost always ignored. The verses were submitted to superficial and emotive criticism, with McHarg interpreting them as "the sanction and the injunction to conquer nature – the enemy, the threat to Jehovah". At least one critic suggested gross exaggerations. To be fair, it should also be noted that McHarg suggested that Christianity was not solely culpable, as other value systems such as capitalism and communism had adopted similar courses. It was also interesting that both writers acknowledged the need for some form of value system. White wrote, "since the roots of our trouble are so largely religious, the remedy must also be essentially religious", while McHarg began a public lecture by saying that his major proposition was that "society needs an explicit metaphysic, a world view which demonstrably corresponds to reality".

About the same time as White's paper was published I came across two limericks that were both humorous and encouraging. The first was written by Ronald Knox, a Roman Catholic priest and writer, who was primarily caricaturing the position of the 18th-century Irish philosopher Berkeley. When included in a book published in 1924, the original verse was accompanied by an anonymous reply that captured God's concern and continuing involvement with creation:

There was a young man who said, 'God
Must think it exceedingly odd
If he finds that this tree
Continues to be
When there's no-one about in the Quad.'

REPLY
Dear Sir:
Your astonishment's odd.
I am always about in the Quad.
And that's why the tree
Will continue to be,
Since observed by
Yours faithfully,
GOD.

Almost 40 years later, and with surprise, I came across another approach to this trio of words while reading about hunter-gatherers in the Canadian High Arctic. Hugh Brody's book *The Other Side of Eden* was published in 2000, but stemmed from the period in the 1970s when he had lived with Inuit on Baffin Island. Brody recounts how his view of the world was transformed by the Inuit way of being. Born of Jewish parents, he also included an examination of passages in the early chapters of Genesis, and offered his commentary on some of the patterns suggested there:

"Genesis is *not* a universal truth about the human condition... Hunter-gatherers constitute a profound challenge to the underlying messages that emerge from the stories of Genesis. They do not make any intensive efforts to reshape their environment. They rely, instead, on knowing how to find, use and sustain that which is already there. Hunter-gatherers do not conform to the imprecations of Genesis. They do not have hope to have large numbers of children; they will not go forth and multiply. Everything about the hunter-gatherer system is founded on the conviction that home is already Eden, and exile must be avoided."

Brody's discourse came as a surprise because he appeared to describe a pattern of life that disregarded a Biblical injunction given to humans. On reflection, I concluded that this is an example of the dangers of taking a literal, and I would probably add, superficial, interpretation of the text. God was speaking in terms that were comprehensible to people within that era and geographical location. They had no detailed knowledge of polar areas or of the communities already living there. God was communicating a principle; and its working out by others, such as the hunter-gatherers of the far north, had to be relevant to location and era.

I had to tussle with these varied propositions based on this trio of words, as well as with other challenges to the Christian faith. It was demanding, but resolution often came by following a very basic pattern of starting with Biblical context and working from there. I concluded that the command to subdue was not a licence to unrestricted exploitation, but a responsible realisation of an authority given by God, to be exercised responsibly with reference to God. In the 16th century John Calvin had recognised the concept of stewardship, and it has been seen as a valid approach by others who do not necessarily work within a Biblical faith, with many preferring to base their arguments on posterity. Whatever route is taken, I then followed theory with efforts to work out a practical, everyday basis for life at the drawing board.

Linguistic difficulties of another sort came when I was asked to design and supervise construction of a new burial ground for an orthodox Jewish synagogue. I met its Rabbi, and learnt from him various points of Jewish practice that should be followed when working on the scheme. It was decided that on each of the two brick gateposts there would be a bronze plaque, English on one side, Hebrew on the other. I asked for the exact Hebrew wording, at which the Rabbi reached for an old envelope and quickly wrote the text. He translated it as "the house of the living Sephardi", definitely preferable to "graveyard".

It was the era of drawings on tracing paper, sometimes with the use of rub-on letters for titles or precise words, so much to the surprise of the office suppliers I ordered a sheet of Hebrew script. I then tried to follow the Rabbi's script, not an easy task as I was not familiar with the letters that had been written so rapidly. I asked a friend who had studied theology to look at my efforts, and a few days later he returned a corrected version. I had not accurately transcribed the "jots and tittles" – the diacritic marks of the Hebrew script. After corrections were made, I sent a copy to the Rabbi with a letter saying that a friend had assisted me, but now it was essential for the proposed wording to be carefully scrutinised before it was sent to the foundry for casting. The Rabbi confirmed that the drawing was correct, and then expressed surprise that a Christian had knowledge of Hebrew.

The unusualness of the situation didn't end there. A few weeks later I had a call from a phone box near the site. In that era, decades before the advent of mobile phones, the recipient of calls could hear money being fed into the slot of the phone box's mechanism. The site foreman had the square bronze plaque in front of him but did not know which way up it should be. Fixings on the back indicated it could only be one of two ways, so I had to describe the shape of the Hebrew letters over the phone to enable him to mount it correctly on the gatepost. The work was completed successfully.

Returning to wider environmental issues, I concluded that a more accurate understanding of "subdue and multiply" would be to see our responsibilities being that of stewards. As humans, we are both part of nature yet also detached from nature, and have been created with real moral responsibility to God for our actions. This was not a new idea – a distinguished 17th-century Chief Justice of England, Sir Matthew Hale, wrote extensively about the contractual framework of man's obligations and rights, accountabilities and responsibilities: "Man was invested with power, authority, right, dominion, trust, and care, to correct and abridge the excesses and cruelties of the fiercer Animals, to give protection and defence to the mansuete and useful, to preserve the Species of divers Vegetables, to improve them and others, to correct the redundance of unprofitable Vegetables, to preserve the face of the Earth in beauty, usefulness, and fruitfulness. And surely, as it was not below the Wisdom and Goodness of God to create the very Vegetable Nature, and render the Earth more beautiful and useful by it, so neither was it unbecoming the same Wisdom to ordain and constitute such a subordinate Superintendent over it, that might take an immediate care of it."

Ten years later I was asked to give a paper at an international conference, and I explored Psalm 39, where David, once a shepherd but later King of Israel, described himself as God's "passing guest" (Psalm 39, verse 12, Revised Standard Version). I looked into some of the implications of this status, and concluded that there were not only rights to be claimed but also obligations to be met.

Others have reached similar conclusions. Professor "Sam" Berry was an ecological geneticist and convinced Christian who frequently discussed the practical relationship of faith with everyday living. In the 1980s he wrote: "The Duke of Edinburgh convened a series of meetings at Windsor on 'the Christian Attitude to Nature'. He challenged those attending with a question: 'There must be a moral as well as a practical argument for environmental conservation. What is it?' The answer, of course, is responsible stewardship, and this is the key to the values that determine our actions towards the environment."

Challenges to faith are continuous, and I see no reason why this will ever change. Going back to the 17th century, *The Westminster Shorter Catechism* was drawn up in 1647 to present a Biblically based faith. It has the opening question: "What is the chief end of man?" The answer that follows is straightforward: "To glorify God and to enjoy him for ever." I am grateful for such clarity, which gives encouragement that there will be pleasure and delight in following the path. This is a far cry from the negative and dour picture of the Christian faith that is too often presented.

More recently, and with feet very definitely on tangible ground, I came across a couple of "landscape relating to faith" examples, both of which demanded thought and illustrated how landscape is involved in many aspects of life.

A friend who lived in Suffolk said that during his travels around the county he noticed that the Methodist chapels were on the sandy soils and that the Baptists were on the heavy clays. He said it lightheartedly, a comment of an identified but inexplicable oddity. I mentioned it to a Methodist historian who immediately responded, "but of course". Her argument was that the Wesley brothers were especially appreciated and followed by the "lower classes", including the agricultural labourers who predominantly worked on the big estates that were on the poorer soils, the East Anglia sands. The clays had been settled and worked by yeoman farmers, and were essentially family units, rather than employers of labour. Yeoman were a group who fiercely guarded their status and rights, and their individualistic nature was attracted to the early non-conformists, often called Independents, who challenged the established church. In Suffolk this movement gradually developed into Baptist churches. Hence, Methodists on the sands and Baptists on the clays.

Another East Anglian episode relates to Edward Welbourne, Master of Emmanuel College, Cambridge, a historian renowned for his prodigious flow of words and ideas. He is quoted as saying: "Why are there so few Roman Catholics in East Anglia? Because it's so flat." Unpacking that statement requires an understanding of topography, sociology, the history of engineering and religious practices. The "solution" is to be found in the 19th century. During the construction of the expanding railway network, East Anglia's relative flatness required few cuttings or embankments and therefore little need for immigrant Irish labour, which had done much of this manual work in other parts of the country. If an Irish Catholic married a local woman, the Roman Catholic church required children of such marriages to be raised as Catholics.

So: *new railways*
But: *few hills,*
                 few Irish,
                         few marriages,
                                 few children,
                                         few Catholics,
all because of East Anglia's flatness.

The second trio of words: Antarctica

The second trio occurred much later in life. I had been at primary school when my interest in Antarctica began, and our daughter was now the age I had been when I had first heard about the continent. So about 45 years had passed, during which time I had been to college, worked, taught and married. The polar interest had always been there, sometimes almost submerged by daily life, but occasionally coming to the surface. Now I was hoping there would be opportunities to return to research work as the fascination remained, not waning but growing.

I took the first small step to begin resumption of polar work by signing up for a conference highlighting specific polar environmental issues. I was having coffee with a friend, and I took the opportunity to ask about the wording of a particular document recently accepted by the nations working in Antarctica. My friend had been involved in the drafting of the measure, so it seemed obvious to ask him for clarity. Within the few pages of seemingly clear statements and proposals, there had been several mentions of "wilderness and aesthetic values". I queried what the understanding was behind the

Satellite image of the Antarctic

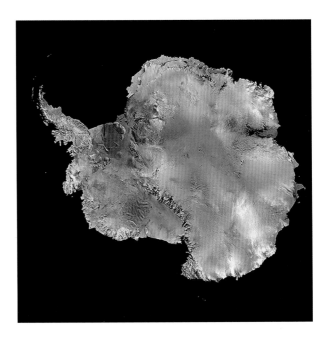

phrase. His answer came with a smile: "You tell me." This second trio of words was to occupy many days and hours of my life for the next six years and result in the second of my visits to the Antarctic.

Since primary school days and the support we had given to the Trans-Antarctic Expedition I had continued to read about the continent, but there were few opportunities to take matters further. There were occasional, usually unexpected, encounters with "polar people", such as an incident during my first full-time job. The office building was cut into the side of a hill, with the staff canteen in the semi-basement. It was winter and had snowed quite heavily so most of us were grateful for hot food in a warm building. As we sat near a window eating our lunch, a figure on skis gracefully shot past our line of vision. A friendly comment was made, "He thinks he's back in the Antarctic", before the lunchtime conversations continued. The skier was a senior member of my department and, despite the conventions of the day that governed the relationship of junior to senior staff, I asked him about his polar work. It transpired he had originally trained as a land surveyor and had five years working with the Falkland Islands Dependencies Survey, the forerunner of the British Antarctic Survey. He had gone South to map areas of the Peninsula and had been a base leader, a post with considerable responsibilities.

I continued work as a landscape architect for several years, and then combined this with a teaching post, so lent over students' drawing boards as well as my own. Again there was an unexpected encounter. I can't remember how the subject was raised, but one student casually mentioned that her grandfather Charles Royds had been part of Scott's first expedition. He had been in charge of meteorological work and also supervised aspects of what now would be called expedition logistics. When retired from the Royal Navy, he ultimately became Deputy Commissioner of the Metropolitan Police and, according to his granddaughter, died when dancing the "Dashing White Sergeant" at a police ball. I have never been able to authenticate her statement but was trusted to borrow his collection of glass slides, splendidly contained in a purpose-made mahogany box, examples of polar photography from the early 1900s.

When I left my teaching post I viewed the break as a self-awarded sabbatical, a time to think and possibly move in a different direction. Once I realised that the pattern of a regular income was going to change, I lived at the level I had adopted as a student – basic food and limited expenditure on everything else. I researched various options, looking particularly at postgraduate courses, using friends as sounding boards to hear my ideas and advise. One married couple listened, before the husband offered the simple counsel: "You can only fall flat on your face." His wife remonstrated with him, but he replied that it was a reasonable position and if that particular pathway proved unsuccessful or unsatisfactory the outcome would not be disastrous. Giving such blunt advice demands wisdom but, even at the time, when I know I was looking for encouragement, I respected his discernment. He was a wise man, and I accepted his judgement.

The outcome of this period of thinking was a preference for the graduate course of Polar Studies at the University of Cambridge. Various hurdles then had to be faced. My initial qualifications were examined by university authorities and deemed to be sufficient, so I was accepted by the Scott Polar Research Institute. Returning to student life, especially in a setting like Cambridge, was a joy. College life was a pattern I had never experienced before, with close contact among students studying a wide array of subjects. A third-year mathematician, who later went on to study astrophysics, put up a notice inviting anyone interested in playing the recorder to contact him; I responded, resulting in a weekly meeting for a couple of hours playing a variety of music. The quartet was completed by a college don who was an historian, and a Russian studies graduate. As for polar studies, seven of us were on the course, four more strongly linked to the Arctic and three to Antarctica. Afternoons were the structured core of the course as we met around the large library table to benefit from seminars led by visiting experts. It was there I met Sir Vivian Fuchs. Our encounter was purely academic as he spoke of the Trans-Antarctic Expedition and answered questions.

Fairly soon after we started mention was made of the final dissertation, the personal study that had to be researched and written up by the middle of the summer term. Initial thoughts were of wide-ranging subjects but gradually ideas became more focused and we settled into our chosen studies. I moved from far-too-ambitious theories of the application of planning patterns to the whole continent to a more manageable study of tourism, past, present and future. I was encouraged in this direction by experienced polar workers, who knew that patterns of commercial activities were expanding and that there would be long-term value in the work. These were the days before the internet and emails, so the early decision to work on a specific subject meant there was time to write letters and wait for replies from different parts of the world. Ultimately the study was completed and, following a well-worn path, I distilled it into a couple of papers that were published in an academic journal. The initial guidance given to me about choice of subject proved significant – it was a case of being in the right place at the right time, and others have since identified the papers as seminal works on the subject.

At the time there were only two companies operating Antarctic tourist cruises, and it was suggested that I wrote to them to ask if they could give me the opportunity of a visit to the continent. One company never replied, but the other responded. When I opened the letter and scanned the single page, I remember being immediately disheartened by its brevity – a mere couple of lines that surely signified a curt refusal. Instead there was an offer of a berth, with the assurance that further correspondence would follow. The trip was the first of my visits to the continent, with the opportunity to see at least some polar landscapes.

Prior to my trip, desk study gave me background to the areas we might see, but there would always be the possibility that visits would be curtailed because of the weather. There was another limitation that was perhaps less apparent. Pick up any Antarctic book published in Britain or the United States and, with very few exceptions, the pictures will be of three areas – the Peninsula, around the Ross Sea or the South Pole. The reasons are fairly obvious – they are where the research stations of both nations are located. However, there are vast swathes of the continent beyond these limited locations. Other nations' research stations are scattered elsewhere, but photographic coverage of the whole continent remains sparse. So, easily available records of Antarctic landscapes are disproportionately skewed, showing a patchy selection of areas.

I wanted to see how the cruise was planned and executed, so did not speak openly to other passengers about my research interests, but the cruise company staff obviously knew and willingly explained procedures. The actual time in the Antarctic was short, about six days. The weather was good and, with the aid of inflatable boats, we were able to land as planned. Safety was critically important, especially as the average age of the visitors was probably 60 or more.

For the next few years marriage and family life took precedence. Again, there was an unexpected encounter with a respected "polar person". "Steve" was a member of my husband's extended family. He was retired from university lecturing, but as a young man in the mid-1930s he had taken part in an expedition to the Antarctic Peninsula. The team was to be there for two years, and they arranged to take with them Christmas cakes baked by Steve's stepmother. Later, others in the wider polar family enjoyed her baking skills, including Sir Vivian Fuchs. As he lived in Cambridge and I went to the city regularly to go to the Scott Polar Research Institute, I was asked to act as courier. So 25 years after supporting his crossing of the continent, and a few years after meeting him in a seminar, I was delivering a cake.

Then followed the second trio of words: "You tell me." When drinking our coffee, the friend and I were talking about Annex V of the 1991 Protocol on Environmental Protection to the Antarctic Treaty, a mouthful of a title, but usually shortened to "the Protocol". In time, the Protocol was ratified and came into international law. The background to the inclusion of "wilderness and aesthetic values" was interesting. A few years before the Protocol and our coffee-time discussions, there had been much debate about potential mineral resources in the Antarctic. The long-standing polar nations of Australia and France had refused to ratify a particular document that included a reference to mining, as the leaders of both countries wished to show their green credentials. Their politicians wanted to reinforce their commitment by suggesting that Antarctica should be a wilderness reserve or some form of international nature area. This was not acceptable to other nations, but in the next major document to come before the assembled group the phrase "wilderness and aesthetic values" appeared, so as to show that environmental issues had not been forgotten.

I benefited from the fact that the phrase had not been thrust upon the polar nations by an outside force but had been demanded by some of the participants themselves. Protesters on the outside of an organisation are at a disadvantage, however

Penguins, people and plants: nesting Adélie penguins and an extensive area of Antarctic hair grass on Torgersen Island, Antarctic Peninsula

strongly and clearly they state their arguments. They have to gain access in some way, to penetrate the system so as to present their case. I did not have to bang on any door, but faced the doubtful privilege of trying to give a degree of understanding to words already accepted by the participating nations.

I sat at my study desk for three years with the hope for another visit to the continent. In time it was confirmed: I would be a "summer visitor" with the British Antarctic Survey. One set of dates was fixed, only to be cancelled because of logistical difficulties, but a slot was found in the following year's schedule. Before I headed South again, I was asked: "What will you do on your first morning in Antarctica?" I stumbled through an answer, which boiled down to saying that I would look at my surroundings. R. S. Thomas's poem would have been a far more articulate response: "Trying to understand my place in it." This described my initial thoughts on seeing a panorama of mountains, snow, ice and sea, broken by islands and icebergs, lustrous in the late summer sun. In time I had to go beyond "my place" in the land so as to encompass a far wider collection of people from many nationalities. I had to marry the theoretical work of the last few years with the actual landscape I was now seeing.

Because the landscape of the Antarctic is so different from other places in the world, with the possible exception of Greenland, identifying its distinctiveness had been an essential beginning.

Two glaciologists described the continent: "The most hostile environment on Earth is Antarctica. In reality, the region is a cold desert, characterised by low snowfall, lack of water, exposure to wind, and soils that lack organic matter"; while a geographer wrote: "Neither natural vegetation nor the handiwork of man can be said to soften or to modify the austerity of a landscape where ice in its many forms is dominant, and where naked rock brings welcome relief".

Geologically speaking, Antarctica is not one continent but two*, lying either side of the indentations made by the Ross Sea and the Weddell Sea. It is approximately

---

*The two parts are often called East and West Antarctica. The following paragraph was included in a seminal book about the glaciers of the continent. I enjoy the fact that a serious, academic study, published by a respected governmental department, can include such a statement:
"In parts of East Antarctica West Antarctica is east, in others west. This of course depends on if you are in east East Antarctica or west. However, if you are in west West Antarctica, East Antarctica is west unless you want to go to west East Antarctica in which case it is east. The same holds for east West Antarctica only in reverse except that if you want to go to west East Antarctica, you still go east."

circular, with a huge mountain range stretching almost from side to side, together with a scattering of mountains pushing through the ice round the rim of the continent. The Peninsula is a 1,000km-long panhandle extending towards South America, with a snow-covered plateau rising to more than 2,000m. It has two distinct margins: on the west, islands fringe the Southern Ocean; while the east is edged by extensive ice shelves.

To cross the continent from side to side is a distance of more than 3,200km (2,000 miles), much the same as crossing America or Australia, or going from Norway's North Cape to Cyprus. Antarctica has been described as a pulsating continent as in winter it more than doubles its size. Pack ice stretches up to 1,100km from the coast, yet this solid but temporary extension is mainly seen in the restricted winter light.

Even the coast is at variance to the usual pattern understood elsewhere in the world. In simple terms the norm is sea meeting rock, sand or mud. Yet, in the Antarctic, this pattern is very unusual, with rock accounting for less than five per cent of the coastline. For all the rest, sea meets some sort of ice cliff, whether "ice fronts" (the seaward limit of an ice shelf), "ice walls" (the seaward limit of a glacier that is aground

South Cove of Rothera Point, Adelaide Island, Antarctic Peninsula

along the line where it meets the sea) or an "ice cliff" (similar to an ice front, but the seaward limit of rapidly moving ice). All are insurmountable barriers, and the only places to land are where visible rocks come to the sea and it is possible to get round the edges of the ice. Sometimes it is impossible to locate accurately the meeting point of sea with land. An experienced glaciologist said that in parts of the Ross Ice Shelf he was unable to define an edge to within 15km (9 miles).

The ice sheet over the land is up to 4.5km thick, representing 90 per cent of the world's fresh water. Precipitation is scant, yet it is sufficient for a net snow accumulation from year to year. While the landscape has been shaped by ice, land exposed after ice retreat has been modified by cold desert weathering processes such as wind and temperature changes. Those who have travelled widely over the continent, whether by flying or creeping slowly over it on the ground, say that the sense of vastness is increased by the essential sameness of the landscape. Huge swathes of Antarctica are unvarying – white snow from horizon to horizon with no discernible difference in any direction. The title page of *The Crossing of Antarctica*,

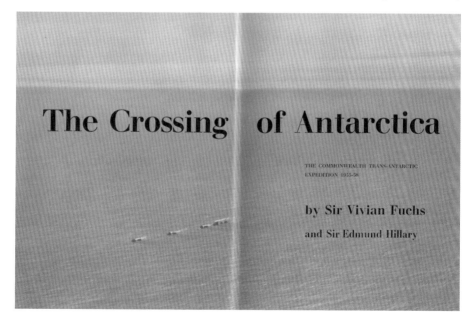

The Crossing of Antarctica

THE COMMONWEALTH TRANS-ANTARCTIC
EXPEDITION 1955-58

by Sir Vivian Fuchs

and Sir Edmund Hillary

the account of Fuchs' and Hillary's crossing of the continent in the mid-1950s, illustrates this clearly. Yet on the continental scale there are differences – features that punctuate these apparently endless vistas of whiteness.

There may be other areas in the world, such as arid deserts, in which vegetation does not make a major visual contribution to the landscape, but in the Antarctic the amount of land with any form of vegetation cover is minuscule. These areas are often measured in square metres, with average height in millimetres. Only two vascular plants are native to the continent, a grass (*Deschampsia antarctica*) and a pearlwort (*Colobanthus quitensis*). Algae, fungi lichens and mosses occur, but growth is very slow, and these forms are easily damaged. "A carelessly placed boot in a mature stand of lichens can eradicate tracts of the equivalent of an ancient forest in a few seconds." The relative simplicity of the terrestrial ecosystem is illustrated by another biologist: "Consider this: one leaf of an Amazonian palm – one leaf out of the trillions in that 3,000-kilometer-wide swatch of tropical forest – may have living on top of it more species of mosses, fungi, lichens, protozoans, mites, and insects than are found on the entire continent of Antarctica."

The French explorer Charcot visited the Peninsula twice in the early years of the 20th century. He wrote popular and informative accounts, and an English translation of the book resulting from his second expedition, *The Voyage of the 'Why Not?'*, was available in 1911, only a year after his return to France. He also highlighted difficulties in judging distances, a problem not usually found when looking at a landscape. He wrote:

The only two higher plants found on the Antarctic continent, the hair grass "Deschampsia antarctica" and the pearlwort "Colobanthus quitensis"

"Nothing is so productive of error as the eyesight in polar regions. The least change in the weather alters one's estimates in truly fantastic manner, and all distinction between different levels vanishes. No polar explorer, I feel sure, will contradict me when I state that it is impossible without a guiding mark to judge a distance in the Antarctic by the naked eye with any pretence of exactness."

He described the sights he saw with appreciation and a freedom not often found in explorers' logs: "The scenery is magnificent. The wild and lofty coast, with its rocks standing out black against the white of the snow and the blue of the glaciers, is magnificently lighted up" (12 January 1909). Charcot's descriptions are echoed by Edward Seago, an East Anglian artist who visited in the 1956-57 Antarctic summer. He wrote: "I had always expected something that was very, very flat and instead of that it was mountainous with tremendous peaks and black rock. I thought there was going to be wide expanses of nothingness and now and again queer upright icebergs and of course I thought it would be colourless; a mixture of greys and blacks and whites, but instead of that the colour was tremendous. It was full of rich blues and greens and the cavities, particularly in the icebergs which one would expect to be very, very dark, weren't dark. They glowed with the most rich luminous blues and greens which were tremendously exciting to paint."

Cape Renard, dividing Danco Coast from Graham Coast, Antarctic Peninsula

LANDSCAPE: A COMMON PLACE

Aurora are not technically part of a landscape but, once seen, they form part of the overall memory of the Antarctic. Initiated by the sun, displays occur when large numbers of subatomic particles from the solar wind enter the Earth's magnetosphere. Wright, a physicist on Scott's last expedition, wrote: "Those who have seen only the pale travesties of the aurora which appear in low latitudes can have no conception of the awesome aspect of the exceptionally bright polar phenomenon – curtains or draperies of fire, swiftly changing in form and in colour, violet and green and red in quick succession and giving sufficient light to read small print." Edward Wilson described his frustrations as an artist attempting to record material as a scientific statement: "As the curtain appears to fold in one direction, it is waved out of sight in another, while the varying intensity of the vertical beams of light which compose it, now brilliant, now vanishing altogether, now stealthily appearing or disappearing imperceptibly, gives the onlooker a strange feeling of expectation and bewilderment, to which is added the conviction that the whole is very beautiful, but quite impossible to represent on paper."

Both of my visits have been to the Antarctic Peninsula. I should have loved to have seen other parts of the continent but that was not possible. I have not seen the polar plateau, but I experienced the crevassed ice field near Stokes Peaks on Adelaide Island, with glaciers spilling down into the Laubeuf Fjord. Before fieldwork, and when sitting comfortably at my desk, I was concerned about the extent to which safety considerations might influence my work and also my appreciation of the landscapes. In Britain, general familiarisation might entail travelling over and around an area, usually by car, bicycle or on foot, often in a randomly structured way – a wander with few restraints. Such freedom is virtually impossible in the Antarctic. Stringent safety precautions inevitably limit freedom of movement. A further thought developed – was perception or appreciation linked to safety? Could the Antarctic landscape only be enjoyed if the visitor was feeling safe or content? When I was in conversation with others about their response to the Antarctic, safety was clearly of great importance to at least some of the visitors, and coloured their feelings and thoughts about the continent.

Anyone writing about the Antarctic faces the difficulties of attempting to convey unknowns. Much later I found a piece by the author Jon McGregor, who identified some of my problems: "With most writing, it's possible to draw on the assumption of some level of shared experience: I can trust that the reader will know what I mean by 'tree', for example, or 'car', or 'cloud'. I may wish to add that the tree was tall, or

Wormald Ice Piedmont near the Southern Stokes Peaks, Adelaide Island, Antarctic Peninsula

gnarled, or bleached bone-white in the frosted light of the sun; but I don't need to explain what a tree is. This assumption of shared experience is how language itself operates, of course, but it's also something which descriptive writing is able to draw upon. But when it comes to writing about Antarctica, the central problem is that the experience of having been there cannot be assumed to be a shared one. Still, after a century of exploration, and a couple of decades of organised tourism, those who have been to the southern continent are in a very small minority. So the writer is unable to assume an understanding of ice floes, or crevasses, or extremes of dry cold, or the peculiar tricks of perspective which result from a landscape without feature seen through incredibly clean air. And the writer is also unable to assume a familiarity with the strange combinations of claustrophobia and isolation which come from living in very small, co-dependent communities a very long way from home; nor of the experience of 24-hour daylight; nor of the effect of vast emptiness on the psyche. And without access to the shorthand of shared experience, the writer will always struggle to push the writing beyond something which is simply 'about' Antarctica into being something which comes from Antarctica.

"Put simply, it's really, *really* hard to describe an iceberg."

One of the members of Scott's team was Apsley Cherry-Garrard, a quiet, unassuming man and a diligent worker who played an important role in many parts of the expedition. Some 10 years after his return he published *The Worst Journey in the World*, an account often rated as the best polar book ever written. He also provided an introduction to another polar biography, in which he wrote: "It has been my happiness to see two of the most beautiful parts of the world. The one was England... The second is the Antarctic. In its grandeur, its vastness and, in a way, its purity the Antarctic is the most beautiful thing in the world."

Cherry-Garrard saw those parts of the Antarctic bordering the Ross Sea as well as the polar plateau, the undulating sheet of ice that covers the majority of the continent and has to be crossed to reach the South Pole. He saw beauty despite the harshness of the climate and the rigours of his experiences. He makes no mention of the concept of "wilderness", but in his use of "beautiful" most would at least recognise a degree of resonance with the notion of "aesthetic value".

Then came a further surprise – the finding of a single word that when used in an Antarctic context could be supportive, even reassuring. The Norwegian explorer Roald Amundsen was also leading an expedition that planned to go to the South Pole in 1910-11, the same time as Scott's second visit. Amundsen reached the Pole first, and successfully returned home, unlike Scott and his four immediate companions who perished on the plateau.

Amundsen and Olav Olavson Bjaaland, a champion cross-country skier, kept sledge diaries on their journey to the Pole, but English translations were not available until 2010 – almost 100 years after the events they recorded. Both Norwegians used the word *vidda*, which is usually translated as "plateau", a seemingly straightforward geographical term, but the translator and commentator Roland Huntford suggests that to see it only in this simple way is misleading. He wrote: "There is no direct equivalent in English. It represents an aspect of the Norwegian landscape. The word means a wild upland, as distinct from a mountain range. It has connotations of untrammelled space. It is also a metaphor for escape... The word *vidda* is deeply anchored in the Norwegian psyche. To Amundsen, the Antarctic ice cap would simply be *vidda* writ large. Using the word in that context would be instinctive. It would have a homely ring, so the ice cap would appear as an extension of his native terrain, and hence lose its power to instil a sense of mythic fear."

Huntford exposed the linguistic and cultural complexities behind an apparently simple term. The five Norwegians could face the hardships of travel across a seemingly endless ice-covered upland with a degree of affinity. The five in Captain Scott's party had no such understanding, and were denied any comfort that familiarity can bring.

Frozen water in the form of ice visually dominates the continent, except perhaps in relatively small areas such as the Victoria Land Dry Valleys. When in the Arctic, Andy Goldsworthy queried whether he was working in a landscape or in a waterscape. Any form of ice, be it on the plateau, glaciers meeting the sea, large bergs or small floes, will in time change, whether in the next hour or during ensuing summer seasons.

Further complications about understanding the landscape came with consideration of weather and atmospheric conditions. Charles Swithinbank, perhaps one of the most experienced glaciologists who worked in the Antarctic, wrote about areas where "for nine months of the year an almost continuous blizzard rages, and for weeks on end one can only crawl about outside the shelter of the hut, unable to see an arm's length owing to the blinding drift of snow". The quantities of snow defy immediate understanding. It has been estimated that during a blizzard day katabatic winds blow 240,000 tons of drifting snow over each kilometre of the Adélie Land coastline. That is an extreme, difficult if not impossible to envisage. When on a short sledge trip on the Wright Peninsula on Adelaide Island we were caught by a blizzard that resulted in us being confined to our tent for the morning, but nothing of the scale that can occur.

I regret that I never experienced "whiteout", the loss of visual perception, usually due to a uniformly cloudy sky over a snow-covered surface. The light is so diffuse that there are no shadows or contrasts between objects. Many are sceptical about it, but the loss of any sense of orientation can cause nausea and confusion. "Birdie" Bowers, one of the men on Scott's second expedition, recounted his experience: "Suddenly a herd of apparent cattle would appear in the distance, then you would think: 'No, it's a team of dogs broken loose and rushing towards you'. In another moment one would be walking over the black dots of some old horse droppings which had been the cause of the hallucinations." In one sense it is the most extreme landscape dilemma because of the total severance of visual relationship between man, land and sky. At least it is temporary.

The clarity of the atmosphere is something I realised only after I had returned home. My daughter was working through an earlier mathematics exam paper, and one question gave "an old formula" for determining the distance to the horizon. I presume it was classified as "old" because the units used were feet and miles, measurements I still use with pleasure. I looked at the most detailed maps I possessed, then calculated that when I was standing on a small hill above Rothera, the research station on Adelaide Island, the horizon of the sea was about 13.5 miles away. But as I stood on that hill, I could see the mountainous spine of the Peninsula stretching into the distance. The peaks appeared to get smaller as they extended down Palmer Land, but this diminution was due to the curvature of the Earth – I was seeing them following the form of our planet and disappearing below the horizon. Taking an average height for the peaks, and the height of my eye-level, I then worked through the formula again. It gave me the figure of 86.5 miles, the distance between me and the farthest peaks, yet I was seeing them with clarity, my own eyesight being the most limiting factor.

I was trying to understand tangible landscapes, areas I could see and experience, but then I read of one Antarctic landscape that is beyond my understanding. It stretches my mind when I even attempt to consider it. A medical doctor, writing about his experiences at another BAS research station, included the comment: "Emperor penguins live in a triptych world of sea, ice and sky, devoid of bearings and recognisable landmarks. Patterns in the ice coastline change every year. Their internal landscape must be mapped with constellations, solar angulations and magnetic contours that give Antarctica a depth and texture invisible to us."

So problems abounded. My experiences were limited, I found concepts that were amorphous, as well as understandings that varied. I was restricted insofar as I have seen only the Peninsula, the finger that points towards South America. I have not experienced the polar plateau although I have seen icecaps and glaciers, but not of the scale faced by Scott and his men. On both of my visits I travelled in conditions that were luxurious in comparison with those experienced by earlier visitors, and used clothing and equipment that provided comfort and gave the best possible chance of survival. But the challenge existed as the phrases concerning "wilderness and aesthetic values" were there in official documents; and as to their meaning, a polar veteran had laid down the challenge, "You tell me". My training as a landscape architect, linked to a long-standing polar interest, perhaps meant I could explain to the polar world applicable concepts from the planning world; and, in turn, inform the wider community, especially land planners, of the extremes and complexities of the southern polar continent. Two years after my second visit, with more than 100,000 words on paper, I suggested a pattern that could be applied on the ground to interpret both wilderness values and aesthetic values. This satisfied examiners, and was offered to the wider world through academic papers and conferences. Despite the laborious effort required to reach that point, my initial wonder at the vast landscape was not diminished.

Over the years I have spoken to many groups about Antarctica and my travels there. One of the most enjoyable visits was to an infants' school. At the time the polar areas were included in the national curriculum for their age, and while I was speaking it became obvious that the children had already absorbed much about the continent. I showed slides and answered questions, asked with great enthusiasm. At the end of my visit I was thanked, and I thought that was the end of the contact.

Then, a couple of weeks later, I received a large, heavy envelope. The teacher had used my visit to introduce the children to the basics of letter writing, and I was sent the results – a letter from each child. The school's covering letter tactfully pointed out the great variations in ability, but I was amazed to see how much had been absorbed. A slide of the dramatic peaks of Cape Renard had been on the screen for brief moments, yet some of the drawings included in the package showed that the landscape had been remembered. Those children are now about 30. They were probably more interested in penguins and whales, or skidoos and tents, than in landscapes, but I hope something remains.

Wellesley First School
Wellesley Ave North
Norwich
NR1 4NT
6.5.97.

Dear Mrs Collie
I enjoyed watching your slides. My favourite slide was the one that showed a big iceberg and a little one next to it ★

Yours sincerely
Katie-Blake.

Wellesley First school
Wellesley Ave North
Norwich,
Norfolk,
NR1 4NT
6th May

Dear Mrs Codling
Thank you for showing the photograph's to us. I hope you cum a gen 'are you going to the Antarctic agam?'

Your Sincerely
From Kyle Daynes

Wellesley First school,
Wellesley Ave North,
Norwich, Norfolk,
6th May

Dear Mrs Codling
Thank you for coming to haer school. I learnt a lot from you. I learnt theat it is very cold

Yours sincerely
Ben Gallagher

Three of the children's letters received after seeing slides of the Peninsula

The Fens and the Wash

If desired, the elements of any landscape can be isolated and listed. Over recent years many have described the features of particular areas, and suggested that in doing so the landscape has been adequately represented. In the case of the Fens, it is relatively straightforward to identify water-filled dykes and rivers or the linear banks and roads running over vast areas of flat arable land. Conveying the sense of space, the deeper character of the landscape, is harder – but for me, the opening of a children's book by Jill Paton Walsh succeeds far better than more complex prose:

> "'We can't be nearly there,' said James, from the back seat
> of the car. 'Here isn't anywhere. It's been nowhere for miles!'
> 'What do you mean, James?' asked his father, driving,
> with an edge to his voice.
> 'No up and no down,' said James, 'and no trees. Nothing.'
> 'It's the Fens,' his father said...
> Under a lemon gold sky the land was black; and nothing put
> a stop to it. Far away on his right he could just see a line of
> very slight upslope; he could not call it hill. In every other
> direction the land ran on and on until it melted, blurred away.
> Before his line of vision was blocked by anything his strength
> of sight ran out, leaving him squinting at the horizon."

The flat lands surrounding the Wash cover more than 1,500 square miles. Now predominantly high-grade agricultural land, drainage of the marshy ground was most active from the 1600s on. Adrian Bell, one of the "walkers with literary gifts" of the 1930s, wrote: "In describing the Fens one is describing a man-made country. Every type of our landscape owes its character in more or less degree to human habitation: even in the wild and hilly regions men have built walls. But no other part is so completely determined by the hand of man as are the Fens. The earth is there simply the raw material of an industry: it has been taken out of the sea: it is a little world which was not, until man brought it into being; and he has moulded it according to his needs... The earth here is black, and gives a peculiar aspect to the day. The sky is clear and bright with spring sunshine, but the earth reflects none of it, it is black as night. It is a curious juxtaposition, the vast blackness of the earth under

Marsh and mudflats on the south coast of the Wash, near Gedney Drove End

a sky so bright, as though the two were cut off from each other's influence." The black soils are derived from freshwater vegetable matter, but to the north silts form the basis of the land.

The poet John Clare knew the Fens and wrote about them, some time between 1824 and 1836:

> ...*There's not a hill in all the view,*
> *Save that a forked cloud or two*
> *Upon the verge of distance lies*
> *And into mountains cheats the eyes.*
> *And as to trees the willows wear*
> *Lopped heads as high as bushes are;*
> *Some taller things the distance shrouds*
> *That may be trees or stacks or clouds*
> *Or may be nothing; still they wear*
> *A semblance where there's nought to spare...*
> *And the horizon stooping smiles*
> *O'er treeless fens of many miles.*
> *Spring comes and goes and comes again*
> *And all is nakedness and fen.*

For a time Clare lived at Northborough, on the edge of the Cambridgeshire and Lincolnshire Fens. Major drainage works were carried out in the early 19th century, and the introduction of coal-powered steam engines consolidated the schemes. Clare would have seen these works, and known about the local opposition to the "improvements". He also thought that such works, together with the enclosures that were progressively extending across the landscapes, were destroying a way of life. It was not just their physical nature, but also the implications for social patterns in the communities based on the land.

Around the Wash is a series of sea banks, each marking a stage in land reclamation. Beyond the outermost bank is salt marsh, merging into the tidal mudflats and the sea, ever changing and treacherous to mariners. Some of the named features in the sea rouse the imagination – who was Peter Black and why was an extensive area of sand named after him? Was the adjacent Bull Dog Sand named after his companion? Both hug the Norfolk coast, while Roger Sand and Gat Sand lie off Lincolnshire. As for the channels between the sands, surely Teetotal Channel demands inventive speculation, let alone two Sleds, Scotsmans and Daseley's. All names on maps and charts, soberly printed to inform and warn, but with unknown and therefore mysterious origins.

Responses to the landscape vary. "There is a strange quality of attraction about the Fens. It is one which only slowly impresses itself on the occasional visitor... There is the strange loneliness of the scene, for all the wealth of its fields." A friend, then a theology student, said: "I like the Fens; there is a somber ferocity about them." I once experienced a manifestation of that ferocity when crossing the Fens on an Ely to Norwich train. We had negotiated the level crossing and the bridge over the Great Ouse at Ely, passed through Queen Adelaide, the scattered community centred around a pub of that name which in turn commemorated the wife of William IV, and were heading east-north-east over the vast Bedford Level.

On the left-hand side of the train, to the north, the sky was clear and blue, but to the south it was a dark dove grey, an ominous shadow hanging over Mildenhall Fen. Suddenly the storm broke and forked lightning fissured the sky. The customary reserve of travellers on an English train evaporated, and those sitting on the left vacated their seats to join those on the south side so as to peer out of the windows. Conversations started and there were exclamations of wonder at the panorama being spectacularly lit for split seconds, together with the sound of thunder which managed to penetrate the carriage and be heard above the continuous noise of wheels on rails. The train rumbled on, we left the storm behind and resumed both our seats and our reserve, but hopefully with memories of what we had unexpectedly experienced.

It interests me now to recollect the books I had read that were either set in the Fens or at least mentioned them in some detail. For children, in addition to *Gaffer Samson's Luck*, there was Philippa Pearce's *Tom's Midnight Garden*, with its descriptions of skating on the frozen river, and Lucy Boston's *Green Knowe* stories, about a house on the edge of the Fens. Perhaps the classic novel set in the Fens is Dorothy Sayers' detective story *The Nine Tailors*, which interweaved the complexities of bell ringing with the intricacies of murder. For ringers, one paragraph stands out:

"The bells gave tongue: Gaude, Sabaoth, John, Jericho, Jubilee, Dimity, Batty Thomas and Tailor Paul, rioting and exulting high up in the dark tower, wide mouths rising and falling, brazen tongues clamouring, huge wheels turning to the dance of the leaping ropes... every bell in her place striking tuneably, hunting up, hunting down, dodging, snapping, laying her blows behind, making her thirds and fourths, working down to lead the dance again. Out over the flat, white wastes of fen, over the spear-straight, steel-dark dykes and the wind-bent, groaning poplar trees bursting from the snow chocked louvres of the belfry, world away southwards and westwards in gusty blasts of clamour to this sleeping counties went the music of the bells."

Sayers not only gives an indication of the method called Kent Treble Bob Major, but also in a few words describes many of the features that dominate the Fenland landscape. Not many towers name their bells, but ringers appreciate those lines. Somehow they capture at least part of the essence of ringing – and for me, present images of the Fens that further understanding.

Waterland by Graham Swift was shortlisted for the Booker prize and was soon found on an A-level syllabus. A nephew had been studying it and revealed he had not known about the Fens, that they were an actual place. I remember my shock at his ignorance, and his surprise at their existence, but my resolution to show him the Fens is unfulfilled as our lives have diverged.

When working as a landscape architect, the Fens were the setting for an engineering design project on the Wash that was to be with me for more than four years during the 1970s. Notification of the firm's involvement came as a cryptic message left on my desk: "We understand that we have been given the chance to do some laundry work west of KL but that it isn't yet in the van." The van finally arrived, and visits to the engineers' headquarters in King's Lynn and the Wash itself became a regular part of office life.

The scheme was to explore the feasibility of constructing bunded water storage reservoirs on the foreshore of the Wash. Fresh water would be captured from the Fenland rivers and pumped to the reservoirs until needed farther south. Then the flow in the tunnels would be reversed and the water distributed where wanted. Engineering aspects of the scheme needed to be explored – what height did the bund walls of the reservoir need to be so as to minimise sea spray contamination? How should the bunds be constructed? There was also consideration of many other issues, such as nature conservation, possible recreational use, effects on local communities and communications, as well as complex financial calculations.

I had lived in Norfolk for about four years and thought I had seen almost all the county by that time. For two years I was in the planning office, and that had enabled me to travel over many of the roads and lanes of the county, but this scheme immediately identified one gaping hole in my knowledge – the fenlands to the west of the River Great Ouse. I had visited the area a few times but was ignorant of the marshlands to the north of the A17, the westwards route out of the county. As for Lincolnshire, the Rivers Nene and Welland – I recognised their names but little more. So for many hours I was reading, then looking and exploring, trying to understand the many parts to the landscape in which I was expected to work.

Shortly after the end of World War II Penguin Books published *Norfolk and the Isle of Ely* by Elizabeth Harland, who also wrote about agriculture and country life. In three short sentences she assessed the impact of the landscape: "Some people find the fens depressing. Some are exhilarated by their vast flat expanse. No visitor leaves them quite unmoved." I cannot agree with the first sentiment but echo the last two. My responses were varied – surprise at the scale of the Wash and its salt marshes and mudflats; pleasure at the variety of plants and abundance of birds; thoughts that living in the Fens would demand acceptance of loneliness. The isolation was brought home to me by a friend, then working in education administration. I was talking of my efforts to get to know and understand the area, and she mentioned that a few children were still being given pony allowances to enable them to get to school as access tracks to their remote homes were too rough for cycling. During times of high winds, others were excused school as crossing dykes on minimal footbridges was considered to be too dangerous. Perhaps only a handful of children came into these categories, but being told about them added to the picture of fenland life.

Two trial banks were constructed in the Wash. The inshore bank looks like a large, long barrow that has somehow strayed into the sea. It is a simple linear bank, running parallel to the shore, grass covered with the surrounding ring of riprap – large blocks of stone, randomly stacked to dissipate wave action. Now they are gradually being absorbed into the sand and mud. It was inevitable that the second bank would be nicknamed "the doughnut". Standing farther offshore, the circular bank was designed to hold water so as to test its construction and efficiency in containment, as well as giving an indication as to the level of sea-spray pollution. Since the 1970s, that bank has become a nesting area for seabirds, hardly a surprising use, given that the riprap would provide excellent protection from wind and waves.

The project's final report came to the conclusion that constructing the banks would be technically possible but at that time the scheme was not value for money. The work was not wasted as much was learnt about construction patterns under difficult coastal site conditions, and that information has been used by engineers for other schemes. In 2006 the project was re-examined but was still considered to be unviable. I have no doubt that regular evaluations will continue, and perhaps one day the national situation or regional conditions will be such that the basic idea will be appropriate.

I was reading a passage by J. B. Priestley, the erudite Yorkshireman whose written and spoken output was both vast and varied. In this instance, he was writing the opening chapter of a book, *The Beauty of Britain*. Not many people have described the Fens as beautiful, but Priestley made a suggestion that I think might be attractive as a way of seeing this landscape: "I believe that swift motion across a countryside does not necessarily take away all appreciation of its charm. It depends on the nature of the country. With some types of landscape there is a definite gain simply because you are moving so swiftly across the face of the country. There is a certain kind of pleasant but dullish, rolling country, not very attractive to the walker or slow traveller, that becomes alive if you go quickly across it, for it is turned into a kind of sculptured landscape. As your car rushes along the rolling roads, it is as if you were passing a hand over a relief map. Here, obviously, there has been a gain, not a loss, and this is worth remembering."

The Fens themselves are not "rolling" – their physical form can truly be described as "flat". The passage was written in 1935 so perhaps "swift" to Priestley might have meant something in the region of 40mph. As at least some of the minor Fenland roads suffer from undulations due to differential sinkage, modest speeds are advocated simply from the point of view of road safety, but maybe there would be greater appreciation of the Fens if they were recognised as one of the parts of Britain that would benefit from Priestley's proposition of swifter-than-foot travel.

For me, the Fens continue to be intriguing and any local news is of interest, whatever the level of information or entertainment. In 2000 the government of the

Inner and Outer Trial Banks on the Wash

"Bored?! How can you kids be bored, with a stunning, vibrant landscape like this to stimulate your young, eager, receptive minds?!"

An alternative view of the landscape of the Fens

day suggested that landscape offered opportunities for teaching and developing aesthetic appreciation in young people. Tony Hall, then cartoonist of the *Eastern Daily Press*, took up the idea and depicted the "stunning, vibrant landscape" that lay before west Norfolk youth. In a similar ironic vein, a "Fabulous Fenland" postcard appeared. The four images are typical of the area but do not convey the whole truth and nothing but the truth.

The last word goes to a friend of both Darwin and Charles Kingsley, Sir

"Fabulous Fenland"

John Lubbock. He was writing in the early years of the 20th century, when wind power was still in use, but before the mass manufacture of the internal combustion engine: "Unpicturesque as the Fens may appear to some, they possess a beauty and mystery of their own. Those who know them, love them; they delight in the long rows of trees, the occasional windmills, the wide expanses which give a sense of space and freedom, the calm sheets of water fringed with tall reeds and sedges and grasses, and the beautiful atmospheric effects."

The Broad, University of East Anglia

Back in the 1970s, the University of East Anglia was growing in both student numbers and physical extent. It had been established on the western outskirts of Norwich, in the valley of the River Yare on land that was once a golf course. Linear groups of mature pine trees, presumably planted to separate fairways, ran along the slopes that drifted down to level land, probably once managed water meadows, but now rough grass, interspersed by dykes. The architect Denys Lasdun used the site to advantage in planning the Ziggurats, the much photographed blocks of student accommodation that also followed the contours of the valley, so as to look down towards the river.

At the time, the main landscape policy for UEA was simply stated – the provision of a suitable environment for an academic community, with value placed on diversity, whether visual or biological. At a very early stage, the development plan included a proposal for a lake adjacent to the river. Several have claimed to have been the first to make this suggestion, and the passage of time precludes certainty. However, I remember that in the 1960s, the period during which the university was established, the city planning department was privileged to have an imaginative and tenacious landscape architect, one John Palmer. Imaginative in that he had the skills and courage to think and develop ideas, tenacious in his ability to enable them to be manifested on the ground. During a casual conversation with him many years later, he said in passing that he had made the first suggestion. A self-effacing person has a great deal of credibility.

Late in 1970 efforts began to try to find a way to construct the water feature. Consideration was given to the possibility of excavation and sale of the surface material, which was frequently called "peat". Letters were written to known peat users, including Bord na Móna, the Irish organisation that at the time was freely developing the Irish bogs for economic benefits. Unfortunately, the coarse, variable material found on site was not of the quality to merit the name of "peat", and it had no appreciable commercial value.

Had the lake been formed by the excavation of peat, it would have been correct to call it a Broad. Until the 1950s the lakes in the east of Norfolk, beloved by sailors and naturalists, were thought to be geological formations. Through a combination of painstaking groundwork and archival research it was shown that, because East Anglia was bereft of extensive woodlands, pits were dug to extract

Early stage of excavating The Broad

burnable material. It was found that establishments such as Norwich Cathedral used at least 400,000 turves in one year, so ideas regarding the origin of the lakes had to be completely revised.

Even though the university lake was not formed by peat extraction, it was still given the name of "the Broad". In 1971 discussion began with a local gravel extraction company regarding the feasibility of excavating the underlying mixture of sand and gravel. In a normal mineral extraction process the resulting pit is usually seen as an unavoidable side effect of a commercial enterprise, but for the university the excavation process was a means to an end, in this case the enhancement of the site. The university was not planning to enter the gravel industry so the agreement with the contractor was on a "no money" basis. It was suggested that a minimum area of water should be guaranteed by the gravel operator in return for the material found. After the discussions, a letter from the contractor went a fair distance along the road to agreement, but left a considerable degree of wiggle room: "The whole operation is very much of a gamble but I do once more assure you that every effort will be made to complete the exercise."

Looking back, this goodwill was evident throughout, and I remember the whole project as one based on trust. There was the minimum of drawings or plans and the maximum of verbal discussion, leading to agreement. I suspect that in today's world such an approach would be unacceptable as there would be an insistence on a formal and specifically detailed contract. The gravel contractor had an existing quarry just over a mile from the university. Machinery at this facility could provide screening and sorting of excavated material, and had this not been available it is extremely doubtful whether an agreement could have been reached. The ease of transport had long-reaching and positive repercussions for the whole project.

Universities are places of study, and many of the students were in buildings close to the area of excavation. Particular care had to be taken that there would be a minimum of disturbance, especially from noise. Pumps had to operate 24 hours a day so these were soundproofed. The river was bridged so that all vehicular access could be taken away from the buildings and on to the lane that led to their existing site. A Bailey bridge was planned and located in a position that would serve not only the temporary workings but also be on the route of a long-term desire-line path. The foundations for the bridge were therefore constructed so that they could ultimately be re-used. Five years later, at the end of the excavation, the gravel company generously financed the long-term bridge that became an important pedestrian and bicycle link between the university and surrounding areas.

Planning applications were necessary, and as the south bank of the River Yare formed the boundary between two separate local planning authorities applications had to be made to both. The Broad, one abutment and about 95 per cent of the bridge were in the City; and the access road, one abutment and the remaining 5 per cent of the bridge were in the County. Having completed and submitted the forms with drawings, we waited. Nothing seemed to happen; there were no phone calls asking for clarifications or notifications as to when the submissions would be considered by committees. I made tactful enquiries, and it transpired that both authorities were waiting for the other to make the first move. Whether it was rivalry or antagonism that kept them apart will never be known. In the end they came together and agreed that permission should be granted.

The gravel extraction itself was the responsibility of the company, but monthly site meetings formed the administrative basis for the whole project. Close cooperation developed between the six individuals regularly involved in these meetings, three from the gravel company, two from the university, and me. Drawings were kept to a minimum, with the site meetings minutes acting as both a record of progress and as the agreement for future actions. The continuity of the employees working on the site was also a major benefit as the gravel company operatives were involved throughout, carrying out the major grading work on the banks before the university's ground staff seeded and planted. Thus the staff who would ultimately be involved in the day-to-day maintenance of the site were involved in its construction. A simple and economic pattern, which over the years showed considerable benefits – high standards of work giving job satisfaction to many.

The extent of the Broad was determined by various limitations on all four sides. A major city sewer ran to the north, the university's boundary was on the east, the River Yare to the south and a designated biological conservation on the west. Despite these restraints, it was possible to enable development of a diversity of habitats, so banks slopes were varied from vertical (to encourage nesting of sand martins) to gentle, together with differing water depths to enable a variety of plants to colonise. Wildfowl required undisturbed spaces, so delightfully named "loafing areas" were provided by a couple of small islands.

The university's requirement for both biological and visual diversity was met by these variations. The north bank was treated as a continuation of the parkland character of the main university Plain, while the three remaining sides were more informal. Even during construction the Broad was an obvious draw for casual recreation – walking, sitting and sunbathing – and when extraction was finished the path around the whole Broad was completed. There is also public access to the site, so it is enjoyed both by members of the university and by residents of the city.

What about the "tenuous link" mentioned earlier? During part of the time the Broad was being dug, a bypass was being built around the adjacent communities of Cringleford and Eaton. A narrow historic bridge crosses the river, and that, together with a crossroads, formed bottlenecks to traffic on the major road into Norwich. The scheme proposed embankments either side of two short bridges before the road was able to rejoin its original line, well past the crossroads. As far as the gravel company was concerned, this project came at the right time. The material being dug was a mix of sand and gravel that was acceptable for the formation of the embankments, without the need for screening and sorting, so loaded lorries were able to leave the university and travel a short distance to deposit their load. The coincidence of excavation of suitable material serving the needs of a major road scheme was an unexpected economic windfall for the company – perhaps the gift of the permanent bridge was a result of its good fortune.

I did not follow the progress of the bypass construction closely. It was a major project, requiring the purchase and demolition of properties adjacent to the line of the new road. The road was completed and the Broad was dug, happy outcomes for many and seemingly the end of a particular chapter of my life.

About 35 years after the completion of both schemes I received an email asking if I had any information about a lady called Elsie Tilney. The enquiry arrived on my screen because I acted as archivist for Surrey Chapel, an active non-conformist Christian church in the city. It came from Philippe Sands QC, a professor of international law who was researching his family history. Over the next few months Philippe and I began to find out more about Elsie, born in 1893 and brought up in Norwich, attending Surrey Chapel with other members of her family. In 1920 she left to be a missionary in North Africa, but in the summer before the outbreak of World War II she was in France. Elsie was asked to travel to Vienna to collect a Jewish child and bring her back to Paris. She went, and was entrusted with a one-year-old baby girl called Ruth. The child's passport showed that she and Miss Tilney entered France on 23 July 1939, days before war was declared. In Paris the baby was handed over to her father, together with an insignificant scrap of paper giving Miss Tilney's name and an address in Norwich.

Now, well over 70 years later, Ruth's son Philippe was trying to find out about the lady who saved his mother's life. Gradually we pieced together information. In 1941, as an enemy alien, Elsie Tilney was taken to an internment camp in Vittel, where she remained for the next four years. During that time she sheltered a young Polish Jew, Sasha Krawec, hiding him in her bathroom for months, thus thwarting his deportation to Auschwitz. This story was unknown to those at Surrey Chapel or even to Elsie's remaining family. A middle-aged single lady, a committed Christian, simply carried on her life without telling anyone of her life-saving actions. Philippe Sands' book *East West Street* recounted much of the information we had gleaned, but we still had no knowledge of the address shown on the paper given to Ruth's father.

A further 10 years passed before we came to an understanding. I was working on other papers relating to Surrey Chapel and was referring to the "Black Book", the rather ominous name given to a register of church members. This particular volume began in the late 1940s when an earlier record had been meticulously rewritten in a copperplate hand by the church secretary's wife. I suddenly saw that the address for a retired teacher had the same unusual house name – Menuka – as that on the paper given to Ruth's father. This house was in a different Norwich street, but by using various editions of *Kelly's Directory* I established that the retired teacher had lived in Bluebell Road during the war. She had later moved nearer to the centre of the city but had used the same house name for her new home. The teacher was almost the same age as Elsie, and other records showed that the two of them had been received into church membership at about the same time. It seemed reasonable to conclude that they were friends. During the late 1930s the Tilney family house was fully occupied by others in the family, so we made the inference that when Elsie came back to Norwich she stayed with her friend and had therefore given that address to Philippe's grandfather.

Visiting Bluebell Road brought the story up to the present day. The site of Elsie's temporary home was now under one of the bypass embankments. It also became evident why she had written on the scrap of paper "Blue Bell Road" rather than the current "Bluebell Road". There, opposite the site where the demolished house had stood, was a cast-iron road sign showing three distinct words. Sadly the sign is no more. It was said to be damaged and was removed, but it is recorded by a photo I took one darkening afternoon.

So various strands of my life had been woven together, spanning more than 50 years. In working on the Broad, I had taken part in a project planned to give people pleasure and opportunity in a particular landscape. It was made possible only by exceptionally close and harmonious teamwork. Then circumstances enabled the easy use of excavated material in building a much needed road – but, in doing so, one of the physical links to a truly heroic lady had been severed. In some circumstances the loss of a material object is disastrous, but my assessment is that losing the building is no major distraction to remembering Elsie Tilney. The events of her life are now more widely known. Her life and Christian faith were inseparable, and she acted with humanity in extreme circumstances, risking her life but telling no one. Philippe Sands sums up his chapter on Miss Tilney by writing that she was "a compassionate woman, not an ideologue out to do the missionary thing".

There was one further twist with regard to my involvement with the landscape at UEA. In the early days of the university, the former golf course provided an enjoyable, but sometimes rather windswept, setting. On the south side of the site, beyond the river, the land rose gently to Colney Lane, a narrow and little used road that linked two of the villages on the periphery of the city.

Present-day Colney Lane with the maturing boundary planting

The university authorities wanted to foster a feeling of belonging, a sense of enclosure, so as to generate the thought that "this is our place". I was asked to draw up a tree-planting plan for this southern boundary. In many ways it echoed the historic pattern of planting around mediaeval and later parks that surrounded the large houses of the great landowners. I suggested a forestry-type planting, using species already found on the site. Oak predominated, with wild cherry, hawthorn, field maple and birch, and also Scots pines repeating the mature groups remaining from the golf course. Planted as small stock, the belt gradually matured. Seen from the university buildings, it fulfilled the original requirement by giving a visual edge to the site.

When planted in the 1970s, the land beyond the university was farmed: a pattern of small fields, mainly arable but with occasional copses and grass for grazing. Inevitably the city of Norwich grew, and with it came the demand for a larger hospital. A site on the west of the city adjacent to the university was selected, and the narrow lane was widened to become one of the main access routes. The tree belt on the university boundary now lines that road, so instead of being only the distant backdrop to those on campus, or visible to the few people using a minor country lane, it is now seen on a daily basis by thousands travelling to and from a major regional hospital.

Hopefully the planting is enjoyed by those who pass by. The design lesson to be learnt is that there should never be a "front and a back", or a "frequently seen and not often seen" aspect, to any scheme. An anecdote is told about the architect Sir Basil Spence when looking at working drawings for the roof of the proposed Hyde Park Barracks in London. The discussion continued until one of his partners commented that several highly paid architects were concerning themselves about the appearance of a constructional detail that no one would be able to see. It is reported that Sir Basil paused before saying, "God will", and the examination of the problem continued until an acceptable solution had been found.

LANDSCAPE: A COMMON PLACE

The Moat

As children, both my husband Peter and I had the opportunity to roam our respective localities, either on foot or on bikes. Peter's haunts included Blackheath in its wilder state, before many of the pits and hollows had been filled with building debris from the London Blitz, as well as the banks of the Thames and the classic landscaped space of Greenwich Park. I had fields and woods close to my home, and bracken-covered commons nearby, with birch, oak and sweet chestnut. Without question, these were the foundations and beginnings of my interest in landscape. Our young daughter was not going to have the same freedom. Living in the late 20th century on the edge of a city, however beautiful, meant traffic and restrictions, so no opportunities for her to wander alone or with friends. It was a loss we recognised and wanted to resolve.

It is now more than 30 years since that Saturday morning when Peter and I were reading the local paper with the first mug of coffee. We saw an advertisement for "a field with moat", and followed it up, visiting the site on an overcast and flat winter's day. There was an added problem as Peter had recently damaged his ankle, and the supportive strapping needed to be kept dry. The image remains in my mind of him walking with a plastic bag over his foot and a loose-fitting shoe – not the ideal way to cross a hummocky field.

These were pre-digital days, so taking panoramic views entailed multiple photographs being assembled and stuck together. The first series we took shows a coarsely grassed field with a clump of trees in the centre. The trees were mainly on the island, which was surrounded by a circular moat, overgrown by vegetation with little open water. A rough causeway linked field to island, which had large areas of blackthorn scrub. There was a single crab apple standing near the northern bank, and a large multi-stemmed ash, the highest tree in the vicinity. It had a heavily scarred trunk, a vertical sear running its full height, presumably the result of a lightning strike. A few alders edged the moat. A road ran along one boundary but there was no roadside hedge, although on closer examination the stools of various trees and shrubs remained, cleanly cut to ground level.

The field and the Moat, as purchased in the mid-1980s – these were pre-digital days, so taking panoramic views entailed multiple photographs being assembled and stuck together

Having seen the site, we made an offer. A local solicitor was in charge of the sale, and sealed bids had to be made by noon on a specified day. This procedure was dubiously interpreted since the bid letters were opened before the specified time. We were phoned and the suggestion was made that we might like to raise our bid "as there is considerable interest", followed by the utterance that our offer was "very interesting". In turn, we found it "interesting" to be listening to a solicitor who was willing to use procedures that could be described as horse trading, wheeler-dealing or any one of a number of terms used to describe questionable financial practices. Our response was that our offer stood for the next 15 minutes and would then be withdrawn. Within five minutes we were phoned back and told that our bid was accepted. The legal process then followed a similar dubious course, with various documentary inaccuracies, but in the end procedures were completed and our exploits in South Norfolk began.

Moats imply history. Immediately available information relating to our particular moat was limited to legal documents drawn up in the 20th century, so reference books covering earlier eras had to be explored. I looked at Hoskins' *The Making of the English Landscape*, but on a quick perusal moats were mentioned only once. The work of the landscape historian who followed Hoskins, Oliver Rackham, was particularly interesting as I knew he was a "local lad", coming from Harleston, less than 3 miles from our moat.

In *The History of the Countryside*, Rackham suggested that moats appeared to be status symbols, dating mainly from the period 1150-1325. Where the manorial system was strong there were few moats, but they were "abundant where the traditions of village communities and open-field agriculture were weak, where there was a multitude of small freeholders or weakly-bound tenants with independence to be asserted". Within the two parishes that make up the Pulhams there are at least 11 moats, suggesting that independence was highly valued in the area. Certainly, digging any depth into the heavy clay demands dedication on the part of the landowner, and strength on the part of the labourer. The area of the island inside our moat is near enough 1 acre (0.4 hectares) and is about 1m higher than the surrounding land, implying that more than 4,000 cubic metres of material were dug and spread.

After reading his book I wrote to Oliver Rackham and received an amazingly generous letter. Generous because he gave numerous references of possible documents that might give further information. In a single page he moved from pre-history to the

The Moat, looking to the island

Planting after about 35 years; and the orchard, with pear trees in blossom

20th century, ending his letter with the hope that it would do for a beginning. Sadly, further research was curtailed as many of the records he cited were stored in Norwich Library: a major fire in 1994 resulted in some losses, but many other documents were damaged by water used to control the flames and have been unavailable until conservation work on them has been completed. So the origins of our moat are still unknown.

In the illustrated version of his book, Rackham writes that "moats are still a mystery and a warning against trying to write history from documents alone", so whatever our actions we document procedures and note finds. One summer we asked a specialist contractor to dredge the moat so as to remove the layers of soft mud and accreted debris. It soon became clear that there was a base of solid, white clay, impervious to water and forming the foundation for the channel. The excavated spoil was deposited in rows on the adjacent grass to dry out, and over the following months Peter raked the material so as to break it down and level the ground. In working through every pile, he found pottery sherds that were carefully collected. These were taken to Norwich Castle Museum to be examined, and later we received brief notes about the finds.

The mediaeval jug base and the unidentified green-glazed sherd

It is known that there was a very productive mediaeval pottery at Weybread, about 10 miles away on the Suffolk side of the River Waveney, so many of our finds were classified as "typical Weybread". The largest find was a jug base, of a size that could be clearly understood. It was far more than a fragment, with a shape that showed the form of a vessel that was probably used on a daily basis by people who lived on and worked the land we now enjoyed. A further piece was fascinating. A mediaeval green-glazed sherd was described by the museum experts as "very odd", with the suggestion that it was possibly part of a water or drainage pipe. A further note on the enquiry sheet said that it had been "shown to colleagues at the British Museum but no-one could identify the type of vessel precisely". I enjoy handling something that has defeated present-day experts. It was carefully made for a specific use, but we are ignorant of its function. A very small mystery, unimportant, yet part of the history of the land.

Purchasing the Moat gave us the opportunity to plant trees. In the early years of our ownership I drew up a scheme using species growing in the locality, predominantly oak and ash, but also hornbeam, wild cherry and sweet chestnut as taller species, all edged with hawthorn, field maple and hazel. Planting these was too big a task for the two of us, so a local contractor carried out that work. With our own hands we also planted an orchard in an area of meadow, using older varieties of apple and pear. Perhaps foolishly, I chose "vigorous" rooting stock, so those trees are now far too high for hand-picking. Much of the fruit is collected as windfalls, but in the near future grandchildren will probably be useful as pickers of at least some of the higher-level fruit.

Thirty years after the first plantings, the Royal Botanic Gardens at Kew drew up "10 golden rules for restoring forests". The moat is in an enclosure that has been in agricultural cultivation for many hundreds of years, probably more than a thousand, so we do not claim to be reforesting it, but the list from Kew makes encouraging reading. We followed all the relevant points it listed – we protected existing trees, aimed to maximise biodiversity, selected appropriate species and tried to plan ahead. Its ninth point made me smile: "Learn by doing". Work on the Moat has taken many days of our family's lives, hard physical labour that has taught us much about the stiffness of clay and the limitations of our bodies. We have had supportive local contractors when essential work was required that was beyond us. The initial mass planting, clearing dykes and removing selected areas of blackthorn scrub were completed by others. In the last few years the work that has given most pleasure has been within the areas of "new" planting, which now stand well over 10m high. I remove branches that have died due to shading from the canopy above; stack dead wood to rot down, as well as providing shelter for different beasties, and have now to make decisions as to which trees should be given preference. Self-sown elders are a continual problem. I try to remove their roots, rather than just cutting them back, but often I am defeated.

Elder reminds me of my father and the story he told from his childhood, probably in the closing years of World War I. My grandfather was a skilled watchmaker and repairer, using very fine and delicate tools that needed careful storage. My father was told he could earn pocket money if he found appropriately sized elder branches, probably with a diameter of about an inch and a half (4cm). My grandfather would cut the stems into sections, then split them lengthways, before placing a piece on his work bench. He would insert the tips of his screwdrivers and probes into the pith, the cork-like centre of the elder, saying it contained an oil that acted as a preservative. Stored in that way, the tools were safe and always to hand.

The 17th-century astrologer, physician and herbalist Nicholas Culpeper has much to say about the elder, listing many uses of its flowers, berries, bark and leaves, but he makes no mention of the pith. Searching the internet, an American site suggested dried pith made excellent tinder for campfires, which links with Grandfather's description of "oil". A British fishing website has chat about the possible use of elder pith as floats, but the idea was not received with great enthusiasm. So I have not found anyone who has used the plant as my grandfather did. I add that memory and my father's account of one of his childhood activities to my "love-hate" relationship to elder. Loved for its blossoms in May and berries in September, but disliked for its capacity to spread and grow so rapidly.

With just one field of limited acreage, I consider that a gentle pattern of management is required. The grass areas are cut as meadows once or twice a year, with additional mowing of a couple of small areas so as to keep the grass shorter for family use during the summer. We have not adopted "rewilding" as a practice. I have read about the experiments being carried out in different parts of this country as well as in Europe, but have not been able to visit any areas. So, as yet, I will not make judgements. Some of the statements made by advocates of the approach frustrate me – it would be helpful if their idea of "nature" could be defined. Talking or writing about "the return of nature" implies that "nature" is, or has been, absent until this or that particular practice has been adopted. When trying to understand "wilderness" in the context of the Antarctic, I read as widely as I could and remember the proposition that only "nature" exceeded "wilderness" in the complexity of interpretations given to the concept. Many books or articles have been written, and oversimplification does not help. In our circumstances, I am happy that in a small area we have taken steps to increase biodiversity as well as greatly benefiting ourselves, as humans, in a multitude of different ways.

Over the years the Moat has had its fair share of incidents, usually humorous but sometimes with a more serious edge. A marriage, many birthdays and a life well-lived have been celebrated in one form or another – all part of the wider pattern of life. Inevitably there have been duckings in water of a questionable quality, but with no ill effects, except perhaps wounded pride. On another occasion a friend brought along a boomerang, a substantial item rather than one destined to sit on a mantlepiece. By early afternoon many unsuccessful attempts had been made to throw it so that it would return. Yet again it was thrown, and on this occasion it began to curve gracefully, heading on a new and unexpected trajectory. One of the party was unaware of its flight and, despite warning shouts, the boomerang grazed her scalp which began to bleed profusely. Our local hospital was in the process of moving, department by department, from its city-centre location to the purpose-built greenfield site – but, fortunately, the location of Accident and Emergency was known. There was a hasty visit to the new and shining department where the wound was treated; as there were no signs of concussion, all was well. However, when in A&E, a lady with a clipboard approached, asking for details of the incident. "Being hit by a boomerang in a field in South Norfolk" did not fit into any of the official boxes, as there was no precise address, no postcode, no police incident number and no insurance claim to be made. Hopefully it provided a little entertainment for the hospital administrators.

As a family, the field we call "the Moat" has been in our possession for a mere third of a century. In terms of its existence the epithet "mere" is fully deserved, but for us that passage of time has been a major part of our lives. Geoffrey Grigson was a writer, poet, broadcaster and critic, and friend of the artist John Piper. He had endless curiosity about the relationship of man and nature, and wrote prolifically about the countryside. "Landscape may exist, rock and tree and red earth, and the shine of water. But it is a very personal affair, the affair of one man and the world.

One man may like to place himself, or his house, cosily in a valley; another on a ridge. One man may need trees, another bareness and wind... Constable had been sensible in saying 'there is nothing ugly; I never saw an ugly thing in my life: for let the form of an object' – he might have added 'landscape' – 'be what it may, light, shade, and perspective will always make it beautiful.'... Constable left things open and free to all of us. What Constable, who was a straightforward man and no clear student of psychology and association, did not realise is how he went about painting himself, how much the 'beauty' of a landscape comes from ourselves, how much in one way and another we project ourselves into a landscape, which then reflects our own being back to our eyes."

A friend described our doings: "Some have an allotment to grow veg, some have a field to grow trees." One particular field in Norfolk has been, and continues to be, part of the lives of four generations from one family. In one sense it is a moment within the historical span of the landscape of the South Norfolk claylands. An individual may, or may not, have an understanding of aesthetic appreciation or a knowledge of landscape history; but, whether 85 or 2 years old, each has made the Moat their "personal affair" and formed their own pattern of appreciation and active enjoyment.

Beyond the landscapes of earth

These thoughts about landscape and the part it has played in my life have almost entirely centred on landscapes and places I have seen and experienced. The size of the sites has varied from window boxes to one of the earth's continents, a vast difference in scale but hopefully still comprehensible. All places have been on this planet, and for that reason within my ability to explore and understand.

The Moon goes beyond this, and I have to question any confidence I might think I have in understanding its landscape. Although we see it frequently, and perhaps even notice and value its waxing and waning, for me it is a different place, somewhere I will never visit. So I read texts and see photographs and films, but it is still a strange, mystifying place.

I have a book, *Full Moon*, given to me soon after publication in 1999. Even its layout demonstrates that the moon is different. There is no title page, no page numbers, no words until the last tenth of the volume. Photographs convey the story of take-off of the Apollo 11 mission, the outward journey taken by the three astronauts, their landing and exploration, then the homeward passage, and the splashdown in the Pacific Ocean. Only then are words used to give data about personnel, the technical details of the photographs and a couple of short essays. One gave information about the flight, but I found that the shorter offering, by the photographer and artist who compiled the book, provoked greater thought. In his concluding paragraph Michael Light writes: "Perhaps what is most interesting about the Apollo saga, however, is that finally it marks a major break from the typical dynamics of historical exploration and territorial expansionism. It is a leave-taking of such unprecedented grandeur and scale that it paradoxically doubled back on itself. Rather than embodying a linear progression to a new world that discards the old in pursuit of endless freedom and limitless bounty, Apollo's path is circular. Humanity's boldest and most audacious movement outwards from its home found itself relentlessly looking in the opposite direction – back towards Earth – from the moment it began." Man went to the Moon, but the intention – indeed, the desperate desire – was to return to Earth, the known landscapes that were home.

The moon landing took place in July 1969, and inevitably (and justifiably) in 2019 the media took the opportunity given by the 50th anniversary to recall the event. One newspaper graphic surprised me. It summarised the actions of the two who landed, Neil Armstrong and Buzz Aldrin, and showed the location of their activities and the routes they took for their walkabouts. Conveniently for both the graphic designer and reader of the paper, all occurred within the dimensions of an international-sized football pitch, a measure frequently used (together with a London bus and Wales) to give an indication of size. The longest straight path walked by Neil Armstrong was the equivalent of moving from the edge of one penalty area to the other – about 65m. In total, the two men were on the moon for about 2 hours 20 minutes, covering less than 1km. I have to admit I had never thought about the distances covered, but simply accepted the "moon walk" as a description similar to "a walk in the park", albeit with more complexities than experienced during a typical Sunday afternoon.

A further surprise came on reading Buzz Aldrin's words: "Beautiful! Beautiful! Magnificent desolation." (Quoted in *The Times*, Saturday 20 July 2019.) Those words are not usually linked as a description of a landscape. I can understand the feeling that it was magnificent to be there, to have arrived and also, in the end, to return safely to Earth. But to me, "desolation" has negative connotations, an undercurrent of despair, so it is not usually associated with anything called "beautiful" or "magnificent". An initial look at the photographs taken on the surface of the moon suggests that "desolation" might be understandable. Seemingly barren craters and plains extended to their horizons – rock and dust, uniform in colour and unrelieved by anything as exotic as vegetation.

But looking again at some of the images gave some understanding of his words. They, too, took pictures of isolated boulders, or details of patterned rocks, as well as landscapes of distant flowing hills. Their coverage followed a similar pattern to mine, when first at a new location. As Repton did, two centuries before, there were "before" and "after" pictures, not of parkland surrounding a country house but of the Moon's undisturbed surface followed by a shot of the same patch, now showing the ribbed sole of a man's boot in the fine dust. It has been estimated that the print will remain there for 1 or 2 million years, and the caption reads: "The image that has come to symbolize [sic] human exploration of the Moon."

Another initially surprising, then sobering, thought was the realisation that procedures had been drawn up to deal with the possible situation that the astronauts were unable to return to Earth. In those circumstances, a prepared statement would be made by the American President. It began: "Fate has ordained that the men who went to the moon to explore in peace will stay on the moon to rest in peace." Putting aside a challenge I would wish to make to the concept of "fate", I was moved by the thought of them having to remain, seemingly abandoned by those who sent them. Apparently

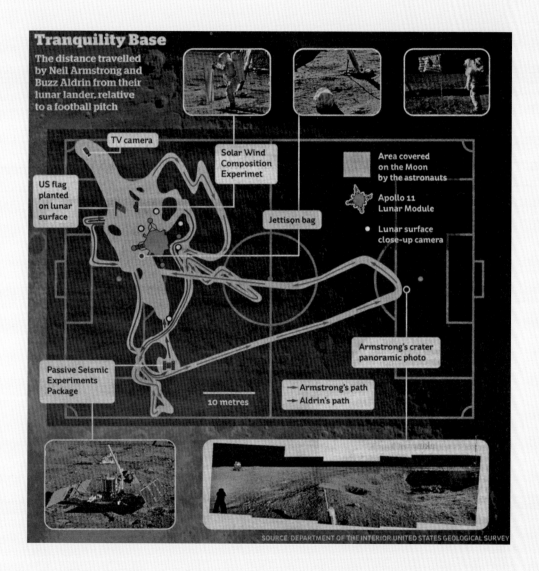

Tranquility Base

The distance travelled by Neil Armstrong and Buzz Aldrin from their lunar lander, relative to a football pitch

TV camera

Solar Wind Composition Experimet

US flag planted on lunar surface

Jettison bag

Area covered on the Moon by the astronauts

Apollo 11 Lunar Module

Lunar surface close-up camera

Armstrong's crater panoramic photo

Passive Seismic Experiments Package

10 metres

Armstrong's path
Aldrin's path

SOURCE: DEPARTMENT OF THE INTERIOR UNITED STATES GEOLOGICAL SURVEY

The longest straight path walked by Neil Armstrong was the equivalent of moving from the edge of one penalty area to the other – about 65m

at the end of Earth communications with the men it was suggested that: "A clergyman should adopt the same procedure as a burial at sea, commending their souls to 'the deepest of the deep', concluding with the Lord's Prayer."

Our use of language, the phraseology we adopt, can sometimes be strange – "magnificent" joined with "desolation", men who ascended high into space being commended to the "deepest of the deep". At first I had no concluding thoughts about the consequences of a failed mission, but then a previous coupling of height and depth came to mind. The apostle Paul wrote to the Christians in Rome: "I am convinced that neither death nor life... neither height nor depth, nor anything else in all creation, will be able to separate us from the love of God that is in Christ Jesus our Lord." For me, that is another surprising, but in this instance amazingly positive, thought.

Whatever our personal beliefs, the moon landing generated wonder and, for those interested in landscape, gave us a truly different scene. So far only a couple of dozen people have been to the Moon, with just 12 of them walking on its surface – although, almost inevitably, tourist visits are being discussed. I shall never visit but will continue to look at the ever-changing passage of our only natural satellite and find it both fascinating and comforting. My thoughts about landscape have been extended beyond Earth, an approach I did not initially expect, but have to welcome as a challenge.

Ending, but unending

The landscape archaeologist Richard Muir offers a warning, based on the past, but looking to the future: "Each landscape is a commentary upon its creators and just as we see the first Elizabethans and the Victorians through their scenic legacy, so too shall we be judged."

That is the judgement we shall face as a community, but on a personal level I am aware that trying to understand "landscape" will be an unending, but still enjoyable, process. So perhaps a quotation by Herman Melville in his novel *Moby Dick* is appropriate: "This whole book is but a draught – nay, but the draught of a draught. Oh, Time, Strength, Cash, and Patience."

Having "found" landscape as a child, its multitudinous facets have been with me for many years – and exploring them has been a delight that continues. In one sense there can be no ending for a book about landscape, but a single verse from Wordsworth gives a suggestion:

> *Enough of Science and of Art;*
> *Close up these barren leaves;*
> *Come forth, and bring with you a heart*
> *That watches and receives.*

Dedication

In 2008 my husband Peter made me a birthday card. It contained the injunction: "Just DO the book". It has taken over a decade for me to distil my collected material and write the preceding pages. In that time Peter died, our daughter Rachel married, and two grandchildren have been born. So this book is for Rachel, Llavan, Alice and Oliver, with the hope they will always have joy in the natural world. It also comes with happy memories of Peter.

Rosamunde Codling

PREFACE
Page 4, "Write the story": Camus, A. 1965. *Notebooks 1942-1951, October 29, 1946.* New York, Knopf. Page 146.

Page 5, "I have looked long on this land": Thomas, R. S. 2000. Those Others. *Collected Poems 1945-1990.* London, Phoenix. Page 111.

MY FOUNDATIONS
Page 9, Map of the Antarctic: *Oxford Home Atlas of the World.* 1955. Oxford University Press. Page 90-91.

Page 11, Cartoon, Hellman, L: *Architects' Journal,* 4 July 1973. Page 17.

LANDSCAPE FOUNDATIONS
Page 16, Stamp: issued 25 February 2003 to commemorate the 50th anniversary of the discovery of DNA. Illustrator: Peter Brookes, cartoonist.

Page 16, "Land is not land alone": Naipaul, V. S. 1987. *The Enigma of Arrival.* London, Penguin Books. Page 301.

Page 17, "There have been numerous efforts": Kaplan, S. in Naser, J. L. ed. 1988. *Environmental Aesthetics – Theory, Research and Applications.* Cambridge University Press. Pages 54-5.

Page 17, "Different people": Ittleson, W. H. and others. 1974. *An Introduction to Environmental Psychology.* New York, Holt, Rinehart and Winston Inc. Page 113.

Page 18, "People attach": Adevi, A. A. and Grahn, P. 2012. Preferences for landscapes: a matter of cultural determinants or innate reflexes that point to our evolutionary background? *Landscape Research* 37 (1) Page 47.

Page 18, "The secret springs of his life": Daniell, D. 1984. Introduction to *Memory Hold-the-Door.* Autobiography of John Buchan. London, J. M. Dent. Page IX.

Page 18, "one who was under the spell": Buchan, J. 1984. *Pilgrim's Rest.* Appended to this edition of *Memory Hold-the-Door.* London, J. M. Dent. Page 301.

Page 19, "In my dreams": Bonhoeffer, D. 1969. *Letters and Papers from Prison.* London, Collins. Pages 71-72.

Page 19, "I was born among the pastures": Bates, H. E. *The Happy Countryman.* 1943, this edition 2014. London, Unicorn. Pages 113-116.

Page 20, "Belonging to a place": Sheila Upjohn. 2011. Personal communication.

Page 21, "The real voyage": Proust, M. 1923. *The Captive, Remembrance of Things Past.* Volume 5, chapter 2.

Page 21, "Know most of the rooms": Fuller, T. 1642. *The Holy State and the Profane State.* Chapter 4.

Page 21, "The Earth should be made": Ray, John. 1691. *The Wisdom of God Manifested in the Works of the Creation.* London, Samuel Smith. Pages 217-218.

Page 22, "In travelling thro' England": Defoe, D. 1724. *A Tour Through the Whole Island of Great Britain.* Author's preface to the first volume.

Page 22, "I have not yet finished England": Brown's comment is said to be in a letter to one of his clients, but I have been unable to track it down.

Page 23, "Descriptive literature suggests": Litton, R. B. Jr. 1979. Descriptive approaches to landscape analysis. In: Elsner, G. H. and others. *Proceedings of our National Landscape: Conference on Applied Techniques for Analysis and Management of the Visual Resource.* Incline Village, Nevada, 23-25 April, 1979. Berkeley, California, US Department of Agriculture Forest Service, general technical report PSW-35. Page 81.

Page 23, "Burt had a keen eye": McBride, J. and Beatty, R. 2007. *In Memoriam R. Burton Litton Jr.*

Page 23, "The hawthorn bloom": Thomas, Edward. 1909, this edition 2009. *The South Country.* Wimborne Minster, Little Toller Books. Page 114.

Page 23, "No human being": Stevenson, R. L. 1882. Talk and Talkers. *Cornhill Magazine.* Reprinted 1912. *Memories and Portraits.* London, Chatto and Windus. Chapter 20. Scott, R. F. Edited by Jones, M. 2005. *Journals.* Oxford University Press. Page 294.

Page 24, "We had the whole of Erebus island": Wilson, E. A. 1966. *Diary of the "Discovery" Expedition to the Antarctic 1901-1904.* Page 175.

Page 24, "It seems to me": Wilde, O. 1905. *De Profundis.* London, Methuen. Page 146.

Page 25, "Landscape is everyone's fundamental heritage": Lowenthal, D. 2007. Living with and looking at landscape. In *Landscape Research* 32 (5) Pages 635-636.

LANDSCAPE AND HISTORY
Page 27, "As in a manuscript": Bloom, Arthur L. 1978. *Geomorphology: a Systematic Analysis of Late Cenozoic Landforms.* Englewood Cliffs, New Jersey, Prentice-Hall. Page 9.

Page 27, "The English landscape": Taylor, Christopher. 1984. *Village and Farmstead: a History of Rural Settlement in England.* London, Philip. Page 11.

Page 28, "When I was your age": Kingsley, Charles. 1879. Preface to *Madam How and Lady Why: or, First Lessons in Earth Lore for Children.*

London, Macmillan. Pages VII-XI.

Page 30, "The material evidence of the past": Hoskins, W. G. 1967. *Fieldwork in Local History.* London, Faber. Page 32.

Page 30, "Constable – that beloved and most English of painters": Hoskins, W. G. 1973. *English Landscapes.* London, BBC. Page 6.

Page 32, "looks like a fact": Rackham, O. 1994. *The Illustrated History of the Countryside.* London, Phoenix Illustrated. Page 14.

Page 32, "The landscape is like a historic library": Rackham, O. 1986. *The History of the Countryside.* London, J. M. Dent & Sons. Page 29.

TWO COMPLEX CHARACTERS
Page 36, "to the same tradition": Wilmer, C. *"No such thing as a flower ...no such thing as a man": John Ruskin's response to Darwin.* The Victorian Web.

Page 36, "deserved to die": MacKay, D. 1973. *Science and Christian Faith Today.* London, Falcon. Page 5.

Page 37, "Analysis of pleasures of scenery": Darwin, C. R. *Notebook M: Metaphysics on Morals and Speculations on Expression.* Pages 36-41. The volume was in use from 1838 to 1856 so the exact date of the note is not known.

Page 38, "It is interesting to contemplate an entangled bank": Darwin, C. 1859, this edition 1968. *The Origin of Species.* Harmondsworth, Penguin. Page 459.

Page 38, "In one study, a single Douglas fir": Sheldrake, M. 2020. *Entangled Life: How Fungi Make Our Worlds, Change Our Minds, and Shape Our Futures.* London, The Bodley Head. Illustration opposite page 199.

Page 39, Illustration of Cambridge Surprise Major: based on the original work by Jasper and William Snowdon. 2011. *Diagrams*. Yorkshire Association of Change Ringers. Page 56.

Page 39, "Gather a single blade of grass": Ruskin, J. *Modern Painters*. Originally published 1856, this edition n.d. Volume III, part IV, chapter XIV, section 51: The fields. London, Routledge. Pages 245-247.

Page 40, "there is a growing pleasure": Darwin, C. R. 1839. *Narrative of the Surveying Voyages of His Majesty's Ships Adventure and Beagle Between the Years 1826 and 1836, Describing their Examination of the Southern Shores of South America, and the Beagle's Circumnavigation of the Globe. Journal and Remarks. 1832-1836*. London, Henry Colburn. Page 604.

Page 40, "injurious to genuine feeling": Wordsworth, W. 1822. *A Description of the Scenery of the Lakes in the North of England*. London, Longman. Page 110.

Page 40, "putting Lincolnshire": Ruskin, J. Originally published 1856, this edition n.d. *Modern Painters*. Volume IV, part V, chapter XX, section 2: The mountain glory. London, Routledge. Page 342.

Page 41, "I know that this is": Ruskin, J. *Modern Painters*. Originally published 1856, this edition n.d. Volume IV, part V, chapter XX, section 3: The mountain glory. London, Routledge. Page 343.

Page 41, "people's backs up": Seaver, G. 1933, this edition 1963. *Edward Wilson of the Antarctic*. London, John Murray. Page 88.

PORTRAYAL OF LANDSCAPE
Page 42, "walkers with literary gifts": Thirsk, Joan. 2000. *Rural England: an Illustrated History of the Landscape*. Oxford University Press. Pages 13, 23.

Page 42, "We were given three thousand lines": Betjeman, J. and Taylor, G. Editors. 1944. *English, Scottish and Welsh Landscape: 1700-c.1860*. London, Frederick Muller.

Page 44, "Blackbirds and the sun of October": Thomas, Dylan. Poem in October from *The Poems*. 1978. London, J. M. Dent and Sons.

Page 45, "one research project": Kroh, D. P. and Gimblett, R. H. 1992. Comparing live experience with pictures in articulating landscape preference. *Landscape Research* 17 (2) Pages 58-69.

Page 46, "environmental psychologists": see, for instance, Ittelson, W. and others. 1974. *An Introduction to Environmental Psychology*. New York, Holt, Rinehart and Winston. Page 105.

Page 46, "A variation of this": Vaughan Williams, R. 1920. The letter and the spirit. Originally published in the journal *Music and Letters*. Reprinted in *National Music and Other Essays*. 1963. Oxford University Press. Pages 122-128.

Page 47, "Painting a bird": Wilson, E. A. (Savours, A., Editor.) 1966. *Diary of the "Discovery" Expedition to the Antarctic, 1901-1904*. London, Blandford Press. Wilson's entry for Monday, 4 November 1901. Page 68.

Page 48, "An Artist Travelling in Wales": Thomas Rowlandson, 1757-1827. Coloured aquatint, published in 1799. Illustrated in Rowan, E. 1978. *Art in Wales: 2000BC-AD1850*. Cardiff, University of Wales Press. Page 116.

Page 48, "He has got some very

marvellous work": Wilson, E. A. (King, H., Editor.) 1972. *Diary of the "Terra Nova" Expedition to the Antarctic, 1910-1912*. London, Blandford Press. Wilson's entries for Tuesday, 15 August 1911. Page 163.

Page 48, "This is a landscape": Berger, John and others. 1972. *Ways of Seeing*. London, BBC and Penguin Books. Pages 27-28. Selected pages from "Landscape" Taylor, C. 1972. *Flikker Book: Landscape*. London, Alecto International Ltd.

Page 51, "Landscape is nothing but Deceptive visions": Walsham, A. 2012. *The Reformation of the Landscape*. Oxford University Press. Pages 1-2. Walsham is quoting Edward Norgate who was writing in 1919 about a manuscript held in the Bodleian Library, written about 1648-50.

PEOPLE IN THE LANDSCAPE
Page 53, "There are figures": Seddon, G. 1987. Figures in a landscape. *Landscape Australia* 9: (2) Pages 107-114.

Page 54, "in picture-England": Nicolson, A. (text) and Meers, N. (photographs). 1992. *Panoramas of England*. London, Weidenfeld and Nicolson. Pages 19 and 28.

Page 55, "to photograph the unphotographable": Weschler, L. 1998. *David Hockney: Looking at Landscape / Being in Landscape*. Los Angeles, L. A. Louver. Page 28.

Page 56, "People have asked": Adams, A. 1983. When interviewed by David Sheff.

Page 57, "give rise to some terrific drama": Morrison, J. Speaking in the documentary *Eye of the Storm* shown on BBC2 on 4 April 2021.

Page 57, "Stepping still farther beyond my own speciality": Benninghoff, W. S. 1974. Macrobiology and ecology in polar deserts. In: Smiley, T. L. and Zumberge, J. H. Editors.

Polar Deserts and Modern Man. Tucson, University of Arizona. Pages 91-97.

Page 57, "The older I grow": Jackson, J. B. edited by Horowitz, H. L. 1997. *Landscape in Sight: Looking at America*. Yale University Press. No pagination.

Page 58, "Values and traditions are clearly crucial": Penning-Rowsell, E. C. 1986. Themes, speculations and research agenda. Summary and concluding chapter in Penning-Rowsell, E. C. and Lowenthal, D. Editors. *Landscape Meanings and Values*. L.R.G./Allen and Unwin. Page 116.

Page 58, "a very fine jungle cat": Macfarlane, R. 2003. *Mountains of the Mind*. London, Granta. Page 262.

Page 59, "Who owns this landscape?": MacCaig, N. Extract from A Man in Assynt.

VIEWS
Page 61, "There is scant evidence": Macfarlane, R. 2003. *Mountains of the Mind*. London, Granta. Pages 145-150.

Page 61, "men go out and gaze": Augustine. This edition 1961. *Confessions*, Book X. Translated by R. S. Pine-Coffin. Harmondsworth, Penguin. Page 216.

Page 62, "The eyes delight": Augustine. This edition 1961. *Confessions*, Book X. Translated by R. S. Pine-Coffin. Harmondsworth, Penguin. Page 239.

Page 62, "very ornamental to the Earth": Ray, John. 1717. *The Wisdom of God Manifested in the Works of the Creation*. Pages 224-225.

Page 62, "I lift up my eyes to the hills…": *The Bible*. Psalm 121 verse 1, New International Version (Anglicised edition) © 2011 by Biblica. Used by permission of Hodder & Stoughton Publishers. All rights reserved.

Page 62, "I used to sit": BBC archives hold several programmes that include spoken contributions from Herbert Howells, and two clips were broadcast on Thursday 14 February 2008 in a BBC Radio 3 *Composer of the Week* programme. Howells called the hill they sat on Chosen Hill. Current Ordnance Survey maps have that name for a community on the east side of Churchdown Hill.

Page 64, "Dad gave me £5": Seaver, G. 1937. *Edward Wilson: Nature Lover*. London, John Murray. Page 7.

Page 65, "At regular intervals": *Daily Telegraph* survey, 27 July 2005. *Country Life*, 18 April 2002. *The Sun*, 1 July 2013.

Page 65, "The Giant's Causeway": Johnson, S. 1779. *Boswell's Life of Johnson* for 12 October 1779.

Page 66, "Nothing is more injurious": Wordsworth, W. 1822. *A Description of the Scenery of the Lakes in the North of England*. London, Longman. Page 110-111.

Page 66, "I ought before this to have replied": Lamb, C. 1892. *The Best Letters of Charles Lamb*. Edited by Johnson, E. G. Letter to Wordsworth dated 30 January 1801.

Page 67, "The pleasure derived": Darwin, C. R. 1839. *Narrative of the Surveying Voyages of His Majesty's Ships Adventure and Beagle Between the Years 1826 and 1836, Describing their Examination of the Southern Shores of South America, and the Beagle's Circumnavigation of the Globe. Journal and Remarks. 1832-1836*. London, Henry Colburn. Page 771.

Page 67, "characterize the

countries":** Gilpin quoted in Egerton, J. 1979. *English Watercolour Painting*. Oxford, Phaidon. Page 4.

Page 67, "Stamps might seem too small": Gentleman, D. 2002. *Artwork*. London, Ebury Press. Page 33.

Page 68, "Characteristic regional landscapes": Held in the Archives of the British Postal Museum, referenced as *Regional Definitive Stamps*. 1960s. A report for the Royal Mail by David Gentleman. Finding Number POST 54/87.

Page 68, "access philosophy": Discussed by Nash, R. 1982. *Wilderness and the American Mind*. New Haven and London, Yale University Press. Pages 242-244. Advocated by Jubler, E. 1972. Let's open up our wilderness areas. *Reader's Digest* American edition 100. Pages 125-128.

Page 68, "For the journalist Paul Simons": Simons, P. 2005. Sunsets on Leek, again and again. *The Times*. 21 June 2005.

IMAGINED LANDSCAPES
Page 69, Postcard: British Museum (Natural History) London. No date. *Landscape Marble*. Postcard DN3.

Page 70, "And now there came": Coleridge, S. T. 1798. The Rime of the Ancient Mariner. Included in *Coleridge: Poems and Prose*. Selected by Raine, E. 1957. Harmondsworth, Penguin. Page 39.

Page 71, "Poetry which excites us": Coleridge, S. T. From Anima poetae. First published 1835. Included in *Coleridge: Poems and Prose*. Selected by Raine, E. 1957. Page 136. Harmondsworth, Penguin.

Page 71, "Fifty years": Codling, R. J. 1984. Polar theatre: two Victorian plays. *Polar Record* 23: (142) Pages 67-68.

Page 72, "brilliantly evocative descriptive passages":

Drabble, M. Editor. 1985. *The Oxford Companion to English Literature*. Oxford University Press. Entry for Kingsley, page 536.

Page 72, "the fruit of my enthusiasm": Buchan, J. 1984. *Memory Hold-the-Door*. London, J. M. Dent. Page 194.

Page 72, "I have been honoured": Hardy, Thomas. Originally published 1887, this edition 1973. *The Woodlanders*. London, Macmillan. Page 6.

Page 73, "One selection": Moore, H. Nine imagined views of Norway 1923 exhibit in "Points of vision", Leeds City Art Gallery. Summer 1997.

Page 73, "survey pattern": I was using a form of Personal Construct Theory, developed in the mid-'50s by George Kelly, an American psychologist and psychotherapist.

OUTLOOKS
Page 75, "For what you see and hear": Lewis, C. S. 1970. *The Magician's Nephew*. Harmondsworth, Penguin. Page 116.

Page 75, "The north wind": Thomas, Edward. Originally published 1909, this edition 2009. *The South Country*. Wimborne Minster, Little Toller Books. Page 47.

Page 76, "Now, when a painter": Sayers, Dorothy L. *Lord Peter Views the Body*. Originally published 1928, this edition 1974. London, New English Library. Page 249.

Page 76, "For over 200 years": Gough, P. 1995. Tales from "the bushy-topped tree": a brief survey of military sketching. In Mihell, J. Editor. *Imperial War Museum Review* 10. London, Imperial War Museum. Page 65.

Page 77, "It may seem strange": Doug Beattie. Tribute to Ranger Aaron McCormick. *The Times*, 18 November 2010.

Page 79, "The wind": Hardy, T. 1878, this edition 1958. *The Return of the Native*. London, Macmillan. Pages 60-61.

Page 80, "musical equivalents": Achenbach, A. 2002. Accompanying note to the CD issued by EMI of Ralph Vaughan Williams' *Sinfonia Antartica*. Vernon Handley with the Royal Liverpool Philharmonic Choir and Orchestra.

Page 80, "letting the landscape lead him": Macfarlane, R. 2010. Foreword to Hudson, W. H. Originally published 1909. *Afoot in England*. Oxford, Beaufoy Books. Page VI.

Page 80, "In the course of a ramble": Hudson, W. H. Originally published 1909, this edition 2010. *Afoot in England*. Oxford, Beaufoy Books. Pages 3-4.

Page 82, "Autumn is here": Personal communication from Maldwyn Morgan, written in late August, no year given but about 2000.

Page 84, "Herbert Ponting, Scott's photographer": Ommanney, F. D. 1969, originally published 1938. *South Latitude*. London, Longman. Page 166.

SURPRISE LANDSCAPES
Page 87, "The water gurgled and slapped": Macfarlane, R. 2012. *The Old Ways*. London, Hamish Hamilton. Page 133.

Page 87, "I keep referring to the place": Goldsworthy, A. 1994. *Stone*. Harmondsworth, Penguin Viking. Page 64.

Page 87, "From whose womb comes the ice?": *The Bible*. Job 38 verses 29-30. New International Version (Anglicised edition) © 2011 by Biblica. Used by permission of Hodder & Stoughton Publishers. All rights reserved.

Page 90, "Over the next two weeks"; and Page 91, "Where agriculture has no place": Brody, H. 2001. *The Other Side of Eden: Hunter Gatherers, Farmers and the Shaping of the World*. London, Faber and Faber. Pages 96-97 and 100.

Page 91, "Inuit use natural signifiers"; Page 92, "Inuit carved wooden maps"; and Page 94, "Until the 1960s": Papanek, V. 1995. *The Green Imperative: Ecology and Ethics in Design and Architecture*. London, Thames and Hudson. Pages 226-231.

Page 94, "Where towns are few": Lewis, C. S. 1958, this edition 1961. *Reflections on the Psalms*. London, Fontana. Pages 66-67, 69-70.

Page 95, "A journalist in The Times": McClarence, S. 2007. The lost villages of England. *The Times*. 13 January 2007. *Times Travel*. Page 30.

SINGLE WORDS
Page 96, "Two academic researchers": Gehring, K. and Kohsaka, R. 2007. "Landscape" in the Japanese language: conceptual differences and implications for landscape research. *Landscape Research* Vol 32: (2) Pages 273-283.

Page 97, "a Welsh word, cynefin": Oates, M. 2019. Nature notebook. *The Times*. 17 August 2019. Lewis, H. 1978. *Welsh Dictionary*. London, Collins.

Page 97, "another Welsh word, hiraeth": Harris, P. 2021. Spotlight on Scotland and Wales. *Impact*. Winter 2021. Page 22.

THE FIRST TRIO OF WORDS
Page 98, "multiply and subdue": *The Bible*. Genesis 1 verse 28 King James Version. A modern translation (New International Version UK) reads: "God blessed them [mankind] and said to them, 'Be fruitful and increase in number; fill the earth and subdue it. Rule over the fish in the sea and the birds in the sky and over every living creature that moves on the ground.'"

Page 99, "the sanction and the injunction": McHarg, I. 1969. *Design with Nature*. New York, Natural History Press. Page 26.

Page 99, "since the roots of our trouble": White, Lynn. 1967. The historical roots of our ecological crisis. *Science*, 155. Pages 1204-1207.

Page 99, "society needs an explicit metaphysic": McHarg, I. 1979. The garden as a metaphysical symbol: the 1979 Reflection Riding Lecture at The Royal Society of Arts, London, 6 June 1979. *Journal of the Royal Society*, 1979. Page 133.

Page 99, "There was a young man": Knox, R. 1924. *Oxford Dictionary of Quotations*. Oxford University Press. Page 403.

Page 100, "Genesis is *not* a universal truth": Brody, H. 2000. *The Other Side of Eden*. London, Faber and Faber. Pages 89-90.

Page 101, "Man was invested with power": Sir Matthew Hale. 1677. *The Primitive Origination of Mankind, Considered and Examined According to the Light of Nature*. London, Printed by William Godbid for William Shrowsbery. Page 370.

Page 102, "The Duke of Edinburgh": Berry, R. J. 1991. Christianity and the environment: escapist mysticism or responsible stewardship? *Science and Christian Belief* 3: (1) Page 12.

Page 103, "Why are there so few": Welbourne, E. 1894-1966.

THE SECOND TRIO OF WORDS: ANTARCTICA
Page 109, "Those others": Thomas, R. S. 2000. Those Others. *Collected Poems 1945-1990*. London, Phoenix. Page 111.

Page 109, "The most hostile environment": Hambrey, M. and Alean, J. 1994. *Glaciers*. Cambridge University Press. Page 151.

Page 109, "Neither natural vegetation": Linton, D. L. 1963. Some contrasts in landscapes in British Antarctic Territory. *Geographical Journal* 129 (3) Page 274.

Page 109, "In parts of East Antarctica": Hayes, D. E. quoted by Swithinbank, C. 1988. *Satellite Image Atlas of the World: Antarctica*. US Geological Survey professional paper 1386-B. Washington D.C., US Government Printing Office. Page B11.

Page 112, "A carelessly placed boot": Lewis Smith, R. I. 1996. Cumulative human impacts on Antarctic vegetation. In: De Poorter, M. and Dalziell, J. Editors. *Cumulative Environmental Impacts in Antarctica: Minimisation and Management*. Washington D.C., IUCN. Page 47.

Page 112, "Consider this": Campbell, D. G. 1992. *The Crystal Desert: Summers in Antarctica*. London, Secker and Warburg. Page 57.

Page 113, "Nothing is so productive of error"; and "The scenery is magnificent": Charcot, J. B. A. E. 1978, reprint of the 1911 translation. *Voyage of the "Pourquoi-pas?"*. London, Hurst. Pages 89 and 82.

Page 113, "I had always expected": Seago, E. quoted by Goodman, J. 1978. *Edward Seago: the Other Side of the Canvas*. London, Collins. Page 221.

Page 115, "Those who have seen": Wright, C. S. 1930. Geophysics. In: Bernacchi, L. C. Editor. *The Polar Book*. London, Allom. Page 38.

Page 115, "as the curtain appears": Wilson, E. A. 1908. In: National Antarctic Expedition 1901-1904. *Photographs and Sketches*.

London, The Royal Society. Page 290.

Page 115, "With most writing": McGregor, J. 2012. Writing on Antarctica. In: Wells, L. Editor. 2012. *Landscapes of Exploration*. University of Plymouth Press. Page 98.

Page 117, "It has been my happiness": Cherry Garrard, A. 1947. Introduction in Seaver, G. *'Birdie' Bowers of the Antarctic*. London, John Murray. Page XIII.

Page 117, "Both Norwegians used the word vidda": Huntford, R. 2010. *Race for the South Pole: the Expedition Diaries of Scott and Amundsen*. London, Continuum. Note 52, page 319.

Page 118, "for nine months": Swithinbank, C. 1988. Satellite image atlas of the world: Antarctica. US Geological Survey professional paper 1386-B. Washington D.C., US Government Printing Office. Page B55.

Page 118, "Suddenly a herd": "Birdie" Bowers, quoted by Cherry-Garrard, A. 1922, this edition 1948. *The Worst Journey in the World*. Page 155.

Page 119, "an old formula":
$$D = \sqrt{2rh}$$
$$5280$$
when D is distance in miles to the horizon, h is height in feet and r is taken as 3950 miles.

Page 119, "Emperor penguins": Francis, Gavin. 2013. *Empire Antarctica: Ice, Silence and Emperor Penguins*. London, Vintage. Page 95.

THE FENS AND THE WASH
Page 123, "We can't be nearly there" and "Under a lemon gold sky": Paton Walsh, J. 1987. *Gaffer Samson's Luck*. London, Puffin Books. Pages 7 and 9.

Page 123, "In describing the Fens": Bell, A. 1939, this edition 1951. Fens and levels. In: Massingham, H. J. *The English Countryside: a Survey of its Chief Features*. London, Batsford. Page 186 and 195.

Page 125, "There is a strange quality of attraction": Shelton, Harold. 1949. Cambridgeshire. In: Mais, S. P. B. Editor. *Lovely Britain*. London, Odhams Press. Page 228.

Page 125, "The bells gave tongue": Sayers, Dorothy L. 1936. *The Nine Tailors*. London, Victor Gollancz. Page 38.

Page 127, "Some people find the fens depressing": Harland, E. M. 1949. *The Penguin Guides: Norfolk and The Isle of Ely*. Harmondsworth, Penguin. Page 217.

Page 128, "I believe that swift motion": Priestley, J. B. 1935. *The Beauty of Britain*. London, Batsford. Pages 2-3.

Page 131, "Unpicturesque as the Fens may appear": Lubbock, J. 1902. *The Scenery of England*. London, Macmillan & Co. Pages 454-455.

THE BROAD, UNIVERSITY OF EAST ANGLIA
Page 139, "a compassionate woman": Sands, P. 2016. *East West Street: on the Origins of Genocide and Crimes Against Humanity*. London, Weidenfeld & Nicolson. Page 136.

THE MOAT
Page 142, "abundant where the traditions": Rackham, O. 1986. *The History of the Countryside*. London, J. M. Dent & Sons. Page 363.

Page 144, "Moats are still a mystery": Rackham, O. 1994. *The Illustrated History of the Countryside*. London, Phoenix Illustrated. Page 177.

Page 146, "the return of nature": Tree, I. 2018. *Wilding: the Return of Nature to a British Farm*. London, Picador.

Page 147, "Landscape may exist": Grigson, G. 1949. *Places of the Mind*. London, Routledge & Kegan Paul. Pages X and 100.

BEYOND THE LANDSCAPES OF EARTH
Page 149, "I have a book" and "Perhaps what is most interesting": Light, M. 1999. *Full Moon*. London, Jonathan Cape. No pagination.

Page 149, "One newspaper graphic": *i* newspaper, 20 July 2019.

Page 150, "Beautiful! Beautiful! Magnificent desolation": "Buzz" Aldrin quoted in *The Times*, 20 July 2019.

Page 150, "and the caption reads": Light, M. 1999. *Full Moon*. London, Jonathan Cape. Caption for photographs 47 and 48.

Page 150, "a prepared statement would be made by the American President": https://en.wikisource.org/wiki/In_Event_of_Moon_Disaster

Page 152, "I am convinced": *The Bible*. Romans 8 verse 39. New International Version (Anglicised edition) © 2011 by Biblica. Used by permission of Hodder & Stoughton Publishers. All rights reserved.

ENDING, BUT UNDENDING
Page 153, "Each landscape is a commentary": Muir, R. 1981. *The Shell Guide to Reading the Landscape*. London, Michael Joseph. Page 17.

Page 153, "This whole book is but a draught": Melville, H. First published in Britain in 1851, this edition 1992. *Moby Dick*. Ware, Wordsworth Editions. Page 147.

Page 153, "Enough of Science and of Art": Wordsworth, W. 1798. The Tables Turned. *Lyrical Ballads*.

I am very grateful to individuals and organisations who have given me permission to reproduce material in this book. Every effort has been made to contact copyright holders, but we would be pleased to rectify omissions in any subsequent editions.

Page 9 Map of Antarctica Reproduced by permission of Lorna Slade.

Page 11 Cartoon Reproduced by permission of Louis Hellman.

Page 16 Stamp Reproduced by permission of © Royal Mail Group Limited.

Page 39 Cambridge Surprise Major Reproduced from *Diagrams*, 2011, by permission of The Yorkshire Association of Change Ringers.

Page 40 The Large Piece of Turf by Albrecht Dürer Creative Commons 467px-Albrecht_Dürer_-_The_Large_Piece_of_Turf,_1503 - Google_Art_Project

Page 47 An Artist Travelling in Wales by Thomas Rowlandson Reproduced by permission of © The Trustees of the British Museum.

Page 50 Cigarette cards 4 and 18 from Gems of British Scenery Reproduced by permission of Imperial Brands plc.

Page 52 Postcards of Erratics, Whernside Reproduced by permission of Jerry Hardman-Jones Photography.

Page 65 Quaker Oats advertisement hoarding Reproduced by permission of Dover Museum & Bronze Age Boat Gallery.

Page 69 Postcard of landscape marble Reproduced by permission of © The Trustees of the Natural History Museum, London.

Page 86 Dhofar Mountains near Salalah, Oman Creative Commons https://en.wikipedia.org/wiki/Dhofar_Governorate#/media/File:Salalah_Oman.jpg

Page 86 Wandering stones Creative Commons https://en.wikipedia.org/wiki/Sailing_stones#/media/File:Racetrack_Playa_in_Death_Valley_National_Park.jpg

Page 88 Icefield on the English Coast, Antarctic Peninsula Reproduced by permission of Peter Covey, British Antarctic Survey.

Page 93 Inuit wooden "maps" Reproduced by permission of Nunatta Katersugaasivia Allagaateqarfialu/ Greenland National Museum & Archives.

Page 104 Satellite image of the Antarctic Creative Commons, author Davepape https://en.wikipedia.org/wiki/File:Antarctica_6400px_from_Blue_Marble.jpg

Page 111 Antarctic Plateau Reproduced by permission of Cassell & Company Ltd.

Page 129 Inner and Outer Trial Banks on the Wash Creative Commons, author Mat Fascione https://www.geograph.org.uk/photo/3331702

Page 130 Cartoon Published in the *Eastern Daily Press*, 30 March 2000, and used with permission from both Tony Hall and Eastern Daily Press/Archant.

Page 131 Postcard "Fabulous Fenland" Reproduced by permission of The Caravan Gallery.

Page 151 Tranquility Base, *i* newspaper, 20 July 2019 Reproduced by permission of www.inews.co.uk

All other images: Rosamunde Codling.

Ansel Adams (1902-1984) American photographer and environmentalist.

John Aikin (1742-1822) Physician and author, brother to Anna Laetitia Barbauld (1743-1825) poet, essayist and children's author. The two wrote *Evenings at Home* (1792-6).

Roald Amundsen (1872-1928) Norwegian explorer of both polar regions, the first to reach the South Pole in December 1911.

Augustine of Hippo (354-430) Theologian and author of philosophical works.

H. E. Bates (1905-1974) Writer with a great love of the countryside.

Adrian Bell (1901-1980) Journalist, writer and farmer.

William S. Benninghoff (1918-1993) American botanist whose work included significant polar research.

John Berger (1926-2017) Art critic, writer, painter and poet.

R. J ."Sam" Berry (1934-2018) Geneticist, naturalist and Christian theorist.

John Betjeman (1906-1984) Poet, writer and broadcaster.

Arthur L. Bloom (1928-2017) American geomorphologist.

Dietrich Bonhoeffer (1906-1945) German pastor, theologian and writer, ultimately executed by the Nazis.

Hugh Brody (born 1943) Writer and anthropologist, sometimes working with northern polar people.

Lancelot "Capability" Brown (1716-1783) Early landscape designer, entrepreneur and effective salesman for his work.

John Buchan (1875-1940) Scottish-born writer, historian and politician.

Albert Camus (1913-1960) French-Algerian writer, philosopher and journalist, winner of the Nobel Prize for Literature in 1957.

Jean-Baptiste Charcot (1867-1936) French scientist, medical doctor and polar explorer.

Apsley Cherry-Garrard (1886-1959) Member of Scott's last expedition and author of *The Worst Journey in the World*, the outstanding summary of the expedition.

John Clare (1793-1864) Poet, writing about the countryside and his sorrow at its changing patterns.

Samuel Taylor Coleridge (1772-1834) English poet and philosopher, friend of William Wordsworth.

Wilkie Collins (1824-1889) Novelist and playwright.

John Constable (1776-1837) Landscape painter.

George Crabbe (1754-1832) Poet and writer, an observer of East Anglian rural life.

David Daniell (1929-2016) Academic literary scholar.

Charles Darwin (1809-1882) Natural scientist, especially in geology and biology. His voyage in HMS *Beagle* established him as a popular author.

Daniel Defoe (1660-1731) Prolific writer of books, pamphlets and journals.

Richard Fortey (born 1946) Palaeontologist and natural historian.

Gavin Francis (born 1975) Medical doctor for 14 months at the British Antarctic Survey's research station Halley.

Thomas Fuller (1608-1661) Clergyman, historian and writer.

David Gentleman (born 1930) Artist, illustrator and designer working in many media and scales, ranging from postage stamps to murals.

William Gilpin (1724-1804) Writer, artist and Church of England cleric, one of the originators of the idea of the "picturesque".

Andy Goldsworthy (born 1956) An environmental artist who creates sculptures using natural materials.

Paul Gough (dates not known) Artist, broadcaster and writer, with research interest in the visual culture of the First World War.

Geoffrey Grigson (1905-1985) Writer, broadcaster and critic, and a friend of the artist John Piper.

Sir Matthew Hale (1609-76) Distinguished 17th-century Chief Justice of England. His integrity and political neutrality saved him from repercussions during and after the English Civil War.

Thomas Hardy (1840-1928) Novelist and poet.

Elizabeth M. Harland (active1930s-1950s) Author, mainly about rural affairs.

Hans H. Harmsen (born 1978) Archaeologist and National Heritage Resource Manager, Nunatta Katersugaasivia Allagaateqarfialu/ Greenland National Museum & Archives.

Louis Hellman (born 1936) Architect and cartoonist.

David Hockney (born 1937) Painter, printmaker, photographer and stage designer.

W. G. Hoskins (1908-1992) Local historian and writer of *The Making of the English Landscape*, one of the first studies of landscape history.

Herbert Howells (1892-1983) Composer especially of church choral works. Ivor Gurney (1890-1937) and Gerald Finzi (1901-1956) were also composers and close friends.

W. H. Hudson (1841-1922) The son of American settlers in Argentina who came to England in his late twenties. Journalist and writer, wandering the countryside.

David Hume (1711-1776) Scottish philosopher, economist and essayist known especially for his empiricism and skepticism.

Roland Huntford (born 1927) Author with a particular interest in polar explorers.

W. H. Ittleson (active 1970s) American environmental psychologist.

J. B. Jackson (1909-1996) Author and teacher of landscape design.

Rachel and Stephen Kaplan (active 1980s-1990s) American environmental psychologists.

Charles Kingsley (1819-1875) Author, clergyman and social reformer.

Ronald Knox (1888-1957) Roman Catholic priest, theologian, writer and broadcaster.

D. P. Kroh (dates not known) American academic researcher.

Charles Lamb (1775-1834) Essayist and poet.

C. S. Lewis (1898-1963) Academic, author, lay theologian and Christian apologist, writing for both children and adults.

R. B. Litton Jr. (1918-2007) American landscape architect and academic.

David Lowenthal (1923-2018) American author and polymath with interest in the American environmental conservation movement.

John Lubbock (1834-1913) Politician, banker and research scientist, especially in archaeology.

Norman MacCaig (1910-1996) Scottish poet.

Robert Macfarlane (born 1976) Academic and writer about the natural world.

Donald MacKay (1922-1987) Physicist working on information theory and Christian theorist.

George Mallory (1886-1924) Mountaineer who died on the north-east ridge of Everest.

John Edward Marr (1857-1933) Geologist, lecturer and Professor at the University of Cambridge.

H. J. Massingham (1888-1952) Author and poet, especially on rural issues.

Jon McGregor (born 1976) Novelist and short story writer.

Ian McHarg (1920-2001) Scottish landscape architect and author who led an influential landscape planning course, University of Pennsylvania.

H. Melville (1819-1891) American novelist and poet, who went to sea as a young man, including time on a whaler.

Henry Moore (1898-1986) Artist, best known for his sculptures but also for drawings made in the Second World War.

James Morrison (1932-2020) Artist, especially of Scottish landscapes.

Richard Muir (born 1943) Landscape archaeologist and author.

V. S. Naipaul (1932-2018) Author, born in Trinidad of a Brahmin family.

Roderick Nash (born 1939) American author and academic in history and environmental studies.

Adam Nicolson (born 1957) Writer, grandson of Vita Sackville-West and Sir Harold Nicolson.

Matthew Oates (born 1953) Naturalist and author.

Victor Papanek (1923-1998) Austrian-born American designer, advocate of socially responsible products.

Edmund C. Penning-Rowsell (born 1946) Author and academic

Petrarch (1304-1374) Anglicised name of Francesco Petrarca, scholar and poet of Renaissance Italy.

Herbert Ponting (1870-1935) "Camera artist" to Scott's second expedition.

J. B. Priestley (1894-1984) Writer, broadcaster and social commentator.

Marcel Proust (1913-1925) French novelist and critic.

Pytheas (approximate dates 350BC-285BC) Greek geographer and explorer.

Oliver Rackham (1939-2015) Academic, an interdisciplinary environmental botanist and historian.

John Ray (1627-1705) Natural historian and writer, ordained in the Church of England, who developed natural theology.

Humphry Repton (1752-1818) Landscape designer.

Thomas Rowlandson (1757-1827) An artist with acute observation, working in watercolours, pen and ink, and prints.

Philippe Sands (born 1960) Author, QC specialising in international law.

Dorothy L. Sayers (1893-1957) Author and poet, mainly of detective fiction.

Robert Falcon Scott (1868-1912) Royal Navy officer and explorer who led two expeditions to the Antarctic.

Edward Seago (1910-1974) Painter in oils and watercolour.

George Seddon (1927-2007) Australian academic with exceptionally wide environmental interests.

Harold Shelton (active 1930s) Author, writing about countryside matters.

Paul Simons (dates not known) Journalist published by *The Times*.

Basil Spence (1907-1976) Architect.

Robert Louis Stevenson (1850-1894) Novelist and travel writer.

Carys Swanwick (dates not known) Landscape planner, originally trained in biology and ecological conservation.

Graham Swift (born 1949) Author mainly of novels and short stories.

Charles Swithinbank (1926-2014) Gaciologist with extensive Antarctic experience.

Christopher Taylor (1935-2021) Landscape historian and archaeologist

Geoffrey Taylor (1900-1956) The adopted name of Jeoffrey Phibbs, an English-born Irish poet.

Joan Thirsk (1922-2013) Agricultural historian.

Dylan Thomas (1914-1953) Welsh poet and writer.

Edward Thomas (1878-1917) Author and poet, killed in World War I.

R. S. Thomas (1913-2000) Poet and clergyman, born in Wales but predominantly writing in English.

Isabella Tree (dates not known) Author and conservationist.

Sheila Upjohn (dates not known) Author.

Jill Paton Walsh (1937-2020) Novelist and children's writer.

Edward Welbourne (1894-1966) Historian and Master of Emmanuel College, Cambridge.

Gilbert White (1720-1793) Cleric, born in Selborne, living there for the majority of his life. A naturalist and early ecologist.

Lynn T. White Jr. (1907-1987) American historian.

Oscar Wilde (1854-1900) Irish playwright, novelist, essayist and poet.

Ralph Vaughan Williams (1872-1958) English composer.

Clive Wilmer (born 1945) English poet, literary journalist and academic.

Edward Wilson (1872-1912) Antarctic explorer and naturalist, trained as a medical doctor.

William Wordsworth (1770-1850) Poet, an innovator in both subject matter and treatment.